THE
CAMPER V[AN]
COAST

THE
CAMPER VAN
COAST

Cooking, eating, living the life

MARTIN DOREY
with recipes by Sarah Randell

RECIPE PHOTOGRAPHS BY GEORGIA GLYNN SMITH

This is for the curious and the brave.

It's for the mud-covered and the rain-soaked, the die-hard, never-give-up campers. It's for those who aren't afraid of a cold snap, a rainy afternoon or a sudden hailstorm. It's for those who understand that there are treasures beyond all wealth in every sunny moment and golden sunset. It's for those who aren't afraid to try something new, who understand the value of simple pleasures: rock pooling, surfing, eating well.

You know who you are. Thanks for your inspiration.

CONTENTS

THE HOW-TO BIT   7

LIVING THE LIFE   8

   What's in season?   12

   Getting ready   21

   Bake to take: Recipes for the road   28

SPRING: TODAY IS A GOOD DAY TO GO CAMPING   36

SUMMER: ICE CREAMS, CLEAR SKIES AND CALM SEAS   96

AUTUMN: PLENTIFUL SEAS AND FROSTY MORNINGS   172

WINTER: COLD STARTS, WOOLLY HATS AND WILD SEAS   240

PLACES TO STAY   299

THE CAMPER VAN YEAR   305

TAKING ACTION: THE WAR ON PLASTIC   310

ACKNOWLEDGEMENTS   312

INDEX   314

How to get the most out of this book

The Camper Van Coast is a book of recipes and ideas for cooking on two rings, with some extra stuff thrown in for good measure. There are over 100 recipes and all of them can be cooked on a standard two-ringed stove, in a camper van (unless specified for a fire, grill or barbecue). But, of course, that doesn't mean you have to restrict yourself to cooking them 'en route', in the great outdoors. A lot of them would make a great supper at home. They are separated into the seasons, starting with spring and ending with a camper van Christmas lunch – although you can dip in at any time of the year.

Sandwiched between the recipes you'll find all the 'in-between bits'. These have been included to give you ideas about things to do, see and play at the seaside. It's the fun stuff. Some of it, like going fishing or picking seaside plants, is food related and is meant to make a foodie trip to the seaside even better. Other entries that are non-food related, like preparing for the first trip of the year, are there to inspire you to fill up with gas and head off in search of adventure. Whether foodie or not, these bits are all about making precious time even better.

At the front of the book I have included a brief guide to some of the better known seasonal foodstuffs and some of the easy to identify but lesser known ingredients you can pick up on your travels. Recipes that use them are included here too. This is because your camper will take you to the places where you can find, buy or pick them at their freshest and best. Again it's all about getting more from your time away.

Of course, along with the fun stuff and the recipes comes a little of the 'nanny state' stuff, the rules, if you like. This is to make it safer, better and more enjoyable. Picking mussels is fun. Getting cut off by the tide is not. See what I mean?

Finally, at the back, you'll find a few ideas for your camper van year. These are the quirky, the foodie, the interesting, the never-say-die traditional and the downright unusual things we do ever so well on these islands of ours.

So, there it is. I hope you enjoy it. Now dip a toe and have some fun.

Martin

LIVING THE LIFE

Fire up your dreams

Anyone who's ever driven a classic camper van will know that the moment when the key glides into the ignition is a moment that's filled with as much terror as it is promise. You're packed up. The planning has been done. There's cake aboard. There is a map on the dash. Yet despite all the forethought and attention to detail, it could still go either way.

But as soon as the old air-cooled engine kicks into life and you hear that sweet, whistling, tickety tick you know that, for a little while at least, you will have the chance to live the life. That's the way with camper vans. They offer so much more than just a drive to the beach. In firing up the old girl, you fire up your dreams. You remember what it used to be like when you were a kid and the summers were long and hot and the days seemed to go on forever. Hope springs eternal. Doesn't it just.

And where are you going to go? Of course it's a day at the seaside. Doing nothing much, feeling the sand between your toes, surfing, beachcombing, eating chips on the prom, building sandcastles, scoffing glorious food, riding on a roller coaster, having fun, feeling free.

It all sounds idyllic, doesn't it? Well, it can be. In between the rain showers and the kids' dirty faces and the tow trucks and the washing up, there can be moments when simple pleasures like taking your shoes off or sampling the gloriously salty taste of fresh-from-the-marsh samphire will make you stop, just for a moment, and take stock of what you've got. It's a good life.

So there's nothing wrong with seeking out a free meal, devouring a mountain of ice cream, cooking simple but tasty food, skinny dipping or jumping off a rock into a teeth-chattering pool. That's what it's all about. That's what living the life means to me. It's what makes me feel alive. And the best thing of all is that, with a turn of the key, I can make it happen.

Are you coming or not?

What's in season?

You don't need me to tell you that eating with the seasons is a very healthy thing to do – for you, the growers and the environment. Happily, it's also a no-brainer when you're in a camper van, driving by farm shops and roadside stalls and a feast of wild food. Other than your dried foodstuffs and long-lasting staples, I would always recommend buying just a couple of meals ahead. That way you'll be sure that your high-risk foods are as fresh as possible and your veg will be tip-top. No one likes a limp lettuce.

Buy food that's fresh, hopefully local and in season and you're practically guaranteed a tasty meal. It's what this book is all about. So you have to shop a little more often. Who cares? At least you won't waste anything along the way. And if you go off-piste and end up foraging for a few mussels, you'll be making an adventure out of lunch. That's the way I like it.

Spring

FRESH IN

BRITISH ASPARAGUS: Season runs from the end of April until the middle of June (weather dependent). *Spring to summer risotto* (page 84); *Asparagus, egg and baby leek salad with creamy dressing* (page 82)

CABBAGES AND KALE: For a perfect colcannon on St Patrick's Day. It's a spring fave. *Chunky colcannon* (page 69); *Colcannon cakes with smoky bacon* (page 70)

PURPLE SPROUTING: From January onwards our world of greens gets that little bit more colourful and very tender. *Purple sprouting with two extras* (page 78)

RHUBARB: After the last frosts, say goodbye to the chills and hello to the first rhubarb of the season. *Rhubarb and ginger martinis* (page 89); *Rhubarb and custard pots* (page 94)

COASTAL PLANTS

ALEXANDERS: March to April, when stalks are young and tender. Peel the lowest stalks and steam them, serve with butter.

ROCK SAMPHIRE: End of April to November. Has a wonderful lemony taste that goes well with fish. Find it on coastal cliffs. *Parasol mushroom and rock samphire omelette* (page 226); *Sea bass with olives and capers* (page 85)

SCURVY GRASS: High in vitamin C, so if you're heading into the wilds, and you've forgotten to take your citrus fruit, chew on this. Tastes so-so and a little peppery. Good for salads.

SEA BEET OR WILD SPINACH: April to late summer. Steam or boil. *Poached eggs with black pudding and sea beet* (page 57); *Lentils with sweet potato, harissa and toasted seeds* (page 269)

FOOD TO FIND

CHICKWEED: Grows everywhere, all year round (check your garden), but it's best when it flowers in early summer. Add to salads, cook in soups, or use dried in herbal teas.

DANDELIONS: The young plants appear in spring and are less bitter than later in the year. Tear and throw in any salad.

JACK BY THE HEDGE: Garlic-mustard flavoured plant. Good for fish or flavouring.

NETTLES: Nettles will begin to flourish in the spring so pick the top leaves before they get too woody. Wear gloves. *Nettle soup with crispy bacon* (page 59)

PRIMROSES: Pretty in salads, pick carefully as wild flowers are protected.

ST GEORGE'S MUSHROOM: From late April (approx). Be careful with the mushies and only pick what you know. *New potatoes with hazelnuts, mushrooms and crunch* (page 157)

WATERCRESS: Grows wild all over the place. Beware, it can contain fluke – only pick it from the centre of fast flowing, clean rivers. *Crab, watercress, tomato and new potato hash* (page 48)

WILD FENNEL: March until end of summer. Use the feathery leaves as a herb to flavour pork or fish. *Barbecued pork chops with fennel, ginger and peach couscous* (page 122); *Fisherman's salad with summer salsa* (page 163)

WILD GARLIC: Grows in wooded glades until early summer. All of it is edible, including the bulb. *Mussels in white wine and cream with wild garlic* (page 47); *Scrambled eggs with wild garlic* (page 56); *Wild garlic pesto* (page 58); *Julia's veggie cawl* (page 68)

FISH AND SEAFOOD

COCKLES: Alive, alive-o. Got a rake? Go get them from sandy mud flats. Delicious, steamed with parsley, chilli, garlic and white wine.

CRABS: Might be tricky to get them from the shore but they are out there. Get them on the quayside instead. *Crab, watercress, tomato and new potato hash* (page 48)

HADDOCK: From the North Sea, best in spring. If you can, get up to Arbroath and try it the way it should be eaten – hot smoked over a barrel (page 183).

MUSSELS: But hurry, because once April finishes, it's all over until Sept. *Mussels in white wine and cream with wild garlic* (page 47); *Campervan paella* (page 166); *Moules three ways* (page 190); *Seafood laksa, for a crowd* (page 234)

SEA BASS: Catch it if you can or buy line-caught for extra sustainability. *Sea bass with olives and capers* (page 85); *Sea bass with a simple fresh tomato and basil sauce* (page 139)

Summer

If you are going foraging for wild plants, berries or mushrooms this season, there are a couple of simple but vital rules. 1. Make sure you get a positive ID from a field guide or are 100% sure that you know what you are picking. Roger Phillips' *Wild Food* and Richard Mabey's *Food for Free* are essential reading. 2. Make sure you have permission from the landowners and don't pick any endangered plants.

FRESH IN

BLACKCURRANTS AND REDCURRANTS: A tasty way to start off your Rumtopf (rum pot) – in a large, lidded earthenware jar, place a layer of fruit, cover with sugar and then cover with rum. As each new fruit comes into season, add another layer. Eat at Christmas. Lethal but delicious.

BROAD BEANS: Great in salads, delicious steamed and served with butter. *Spring to summer risotto* (page 84); *One pan lamb with peas, broad beans and mint* (page 165)

FRESH PEAS: Find a quiet spot and shell them in the sun. Don't eat too many. *Spring to summer risotto* (page 84); *One pan lamb with peas, broad beans and mint* (page 165)

NEW SPUDS: Perfect for salads or try the *Canarian seawater spuds with a green mojo dip* (page 158)

STRAWBERRIES: Once you've picked your own, or grown your own, the out of season varieties will never taste the same. Tiny wild ones are a treat. *Strawberries and raspberries with zesty sugar* (page 171); *Strawberry 'mess'* (page 170)

COASTAL PLANTS

DULSE: Gorgeous red seaweed that can be chewed raw, as a snack (page 51).

MARSH SAMPHIRE: The ultimate seaside-tasting treat. Served in posh restaurants by top chefs, foraged by you on muddy tidal banks. Boil for 3-4 minutes, toss in olive oil and lemon juice and eat with a good piece of grilled fish.
SEA LETTUCE: Thin, green seaweed sheets that can be eaten raw.
SUGAR KELP: Picked on low spring tides. Can be used as a pasta substitute, for wrapping fish to steam or dried as crisps. *Sugar kelp crisps, camper van style* (page 53)
SEA PURSLANE: The edible leaves grow on muddy estuaries and can be eaten raw or boiled as a veg.

FOOD TO FIND

CHAMOMILE: These daisy-like wonder flowers are used as an anti-inflammatory and even help with rheumatism and arthritis. The flowers are edible too and make a great, soothing cuppa. *A tea for the autumn* (page 238)
CHANTERELLES: Take care when picking that you've got it right. Delicious fried in butter or with milk. *New potatoes with hazelnuts, mushrooms and crunch* (page 157)
ELDERFLOWER: Divine in tempura batter. Also good for cordial. *Poached greenages or apricots with lemon and lime cream* (page 169)
GOOSEBERRIES: Arguably the devil's fruit. Give them a wide berth, or pick them in the wild and make a compote.
MEADOWSWEET: A beautifully fragrant plant traditionally used for making houses smell nice. Put some in the awning or make cordial. Boil up the flowering heads with sugar and lemon juice, strain and bottle.

FISH AND SEAFOOD

LOBSTER: If you get lucky, make sure it's at least 90mm along its carapace from eye socket to tail (don't include the tail). Use a gaff made with bamboo and an old coat hanger to get them out of their hidey-holes. *Barbecued lobster with Thai flavours* (page 127)
MACKEREL: The further south you are, the more likely you'll get the early arrivals. Summer bonanza. *Mackerel, 5 ways* (page 179)
PRAWNS AND SHRIMP: Use a push net to stir up the common shrimp from sandy beaches or a dip net to tease prawns out of the seaweed. *Fisherman's salad with summer salsa* (page 163); *Seafood laksa, for a crowd* (page 234); *Fraser's patented prawn catcher* (page 189)
VELVET SWIMMERS: Feisty, fiddly and not for the faint-hearted. But delicious. *Simple velvet swimmer crab with pasta* (page 187)

Autumn

Autumn is harvest time for the farmers. It's also a pretty good time to be on the coast, with a few of the coastal wonders left to gather. Sea beet and rock samphire will still be good and mussels come back on to the menu after a summer of spawning.

FRESH IN

APPLES: If you are a nine-year-old boy living in 1950s Somerset, scrump them if you can. Otherwise, buy British. *Pork, scrumpy, apple and fennel pot roast* (page 237)

CELERIAC: Underused, but makes fresh-tasting mash and great for autumn stews. *Celeriac, crispy bacon and parsley couscous risotto* (page 229); *Duck breasts with ginger and orange with celeriac mash* (page 275)

ONIONS: Whilst you can get them any time of the year now is the time for the new season. Perfect for onion soup to warm you up on a chilly autumn evening. *French onion soup with cheesy croutes* (page 228)

PARSNIP: For that close-to-Christmas feeling. *Root veggies with chestnuts and parsley* (page 293); *Winter veg crisps* (page 267)

FOOD TO FIND

BLACKBERRIES: The classic forage. Eat them on the hoof before the birdies do, or for something different, try Sarah's *Blackberry lime fizz* (page 238)

ELDERBERRIES: Boil up with sugar to make an easy and cheap cordial.

HAZELNUTS: You know the drill. Get there before the squirrels do. *Purple sprouting with two extras* (page 78); *New potatoes with hazelnuts, mushrooms and crunch* (page 157)

PARASOL MUSHROOMS: We have found giants of these on coastal walks in open pasture. Identify carefully. Fry in butter with dried thyme and black pepper. It's tempting to take them all, but don't. Only what you need. *Parasol mushroom and rock samphire omelette* (page 226)

PUFFBALL MUSHROOMS: The legendary puffballs can be fried like steak, or used like any other mushroom as long as the flesh is still white. Again, act with caution.

ROSE HIPS: Deseed, dry them on the dashboard then infuse in hot water for a healthy, caffeine-free tea.

SLOES: Ready for the run-up to Christmas, soak sugar and sloes in gin and wait...

SWEET CHESTNUTS: Getting in the mood for winter? Roast them over a beach fire and you'll be ready. *Roasting chestnuts on a beach fire* (page 261); *Root veggies with chestnuts and parsley* (page 293)

FISH AND SEAFOOD

JOHN DORY: Light and fresh, fry fillets in butter for a subtle and delicious fishy taste.

LIMPETS: Curious? Steam them in their own juices topped with gut weed, over a beach fire.

MACKEREL: Here we go again. My all-time fave; line-caught it's a sustainable, guilt-free treat. For added excitement, try smoking. *Easy smoked mackerel pâté on toast with radishes* (page 185)

MUSSELS: Steamed in foil over a fire? Nothing better. Get them on low spring tides on beaches that are pollution-free. De-grit and plump them with a handful of oats in fresh water, or use a dash of vinegar in fresh water. I don't know why, but it works.

OYSTERS: With Guinness? Why not. Some say the best way to eat them is raw, quickly, with lemon and a pinch of pepper.

SCALLOPS: Another beautiful shellfish that's versatile and delicious: pan-fried, barbecued, whatever. Hand-picked rather than dredged any day. Costly, but worth it. *Scallops with garam masala butter* (page 88); *Fisherman's salad with summer salsa* (page 163)

Winter

In winter it all goes a bit quiet. We still enjoy the odd mussel feast in our van, as well as an occasional foray for crabs – though by this time, most of them will have retreated. There are prizes to be enjoyed, however, once you know what to find.

FRESH IN

BEETROOT: Fresh beetroot adds a gorgeous earthy taste to any meal and it's great for making crisps. *Winter veg crisps* (page 267)

BRUSSELS SPROUTS: In the confines of a small van, with their reputation, use sparingly. *Essential buttery sprouts* (page 293)

PARSNIPS: Slice and fry = perfect crisps. *Julia's veggie cawl* (page 68);
Winter veg crisps (page 267)
WINTER GREENS: Boiled and then fried with cream and bacon, oh yes.

FOOD TO FIND

ALEXANDERS: One of the first umbellifers to come up in the late winter.
Recognisable by its yellow flowers and broad waxy leaves. Tastes somewhere
between celery and parsley.
WILD CABBAGE: Beautiful-looking plant that I've seen in South Wales as well
as on the south coast of England. Boil young leaves like cabbage. Or simply enjoy it
where it is.

FISH AND SEAFOOD

COCKLES: It's a little cold to feel for them in muddy estuaries with your feet at
this time of year but try raking them out. Use the head of the rake to agitate the
sand, then, when it begins to turn liquid, rake them out.
DOG WHELKS: These little carnivorous snails of the sea aren't to everyone's taste,
but they make an interesting snack if you've got a fire on the go. You'll need a pin
to get the flesh out. Boil then fry them in a little butter. Make sure the sea is clean.
RAZOR CLAMS: The elusive foraging prize! I search on, ever hopeful. Low spring
tides and a packet of salt is what you'll need. Sprinkle on the figure-of-eight shaped
holes and grab as they pop up.

Getting ready

So the sun comes out and you're ready to go camping.
Excellent! I've always said that preparation is everything
when it comes to going away in a camper, whatever the time
of year it is. And it is. Along with spontaneity, luck, a sense
of humour and a following wind. It's not too much to ask, is it?

Coming out of hibernation

Thinking about the first trip of the year always fills me with excitement. I spend
days, weeks even, getting the van ready, packing everything in and making sure
we've got everything we need. It's all done lovingly, with the prospect of exciting
adventures ahead. It's a good time to be a van.

One of the best things about a camper is that the camping year can start so much
sooner. Without having to worry about cold nights and bad weather so much as our
tented friends, we can set off earlier. But don't rush for the wild blue yonder without
taking a few minutes (at the very least) to make sure that both you and your van have
survived the winter. If you follow the storage advice on page 246, then your van should
emerge like a shiny, chrome-bumpered butterfly into the bright spring sunshine.

For a quick getaway, check:
★ The cables haven't seized up.
★ The tyre pressure.
★ The oil level.
★ The rubber pipes aren't leaking gas (if you can, get the gas man to take a peek).
★ The electric hook-up is working (again, if you know a friendly electrician . . .).
★ The handbrake hasn't seized on.
★ The lights (including interior lights) are working.
★ The brake fluid levels.
★ The windscreen washer levels.
★ The leisure battery is charged and the batteries on the carbon monoxide
   alarm are tested.

★ The hinges and moving parts on the elevating roof (if you have one) have not seized up.

★ Finally, check that you've got enough gas to cook your first meal and you won't have half-heated beans again.

If you are the slightest bit concerned about any of the above, I'd recommend getting the van serviced before you head off. Just to be sure.

Camper van food storage

How's your fridge? If it's anything like mine then its performance will be sporadic at best. Most fridges will run off battery power or gas, so you've got to remember to switch over when you drive or park up. And lighting them isn't always easy. The point is, you can never tell how well your food is storing, compared with at home. So high-risk foods, such as eggs, meat, fish and dairy produce, should be bought just before you intend to use them. Don't rush off to the shops and do it all before you leave, unless you are sure your fridge is up to the job. Likewise, if you have a cooler.

Storing food that's been opened is OK, so long as it's covered, not kept for more than a couple of days and below 8°C. Tins, of course, should be decanted into non-metal containers. So if you can't resist a tin of beans *and* can't finish it (can't think how that could happen), keep the rest in a Tupperware dish and chuck it in the cooler.

PREPARATION
It always makes sense to make time for a spring clean and a refresh of your cupboard contents. What's lurking at the back? How long has it been there? Is it alive? Are you well stocked with dried and long-lasting staples? You don't want to starve if you hit hot weather and the fridge fails.

Kitchen essentials
★ Couscous (add peppers, courgette, nuts and some herbs for a tasty emergency snack)
★ Pasta (in an emergency a tin of tomatoes and some basil and garlic will do)
★ Rice (for risotto, paella, rice pudding or pilaf)
★ Jar of pesto and some dried herbs

- ★ A few tins (baked beans, kidney beans, butter beans, chick peas and tomatoes)
- ★ Fajitas (use instead of buns, will keep for a few days longer than bread)
- ★ Chorizo (lasts well and is great with just about anything)
- ★ Garlic, onions, bay leaves and stock cubes
- ★ Olive oil
- ★ Flour and caster sugar, salt and pepper
- ★ Tea bags (and the rest)

Stuff to stash

My friend Cath has a great way of being ready for trips away and that's to have duplicates of useful stuff like toothbrushes, toothpaste and shampoo in the van at the start of the season. It means she doesn't have to scrabble around finding everyone's bits and pieces before they leave.

This wash bag theory also extends to sleeping bags, pillows (unless you have a favourite you can't sleep without) and any other essentials that won't go off. If the kids have a spare teddy, or doo-doo or whatever they call it, stash him in the van.

STAY FIT WITH A GOOD FIRST AID KIT

No brainer? You'd think so. A few steri strips, a bandage or two and a selection of plasters will come in useful at some point or other. More important, though, are items like sun cream, antiseptic cream, tea tree oil, insect repellent and antihistamine. Also, consider having a week's supply of any medication you might need in the van (as long as it doesn't go off). This will serve a double purpose. If you run out at home, you'll have a spare and you won't have to go through the hassle of getting more before you leave.

Cool weather camping clobber

'There's no such thing as bad weather, just bad clothing…'

One thing that's certain about camping in the UK is that you never know what's going to happen weatherwise. Daytime can bring anything from hail and thunder to blistering sunshine. And it can sure get chilly at night. If you're going to be active in varying temperatures, you'll need more than a t-shirt and big heavy coat, a combination that has only two heat settings: boiling hot and freezing cold. So it's time to do a bit of layering.

BASE LAYER: The layer next to your skin needs to provide warmth, be able to breathe, dry quickly and wick moisture away from your skin. Forget cotton and polyester and invest in some Merino wool. Wool increases in temperature by three degrees when wet and its antibacterial qualities will stop it (and you) smelling, meaning you can wear it day and night – perfect for camping! Silk and bamboo are similarly natural and sustainable, and Tencel and Modal are fine fabrics too.

MID LAYER: This is the bit which keeps you warm and which you shed if you get hot. Go for fleece or wool, depending on what you're up to. With wool, you can go thinner, meaning it'll be light enough to stuff in a day-pack if you take it off. Again, natural fibres have all those wonderful wicking and thermal properties, but without the stink.

OUTER LAYER: This is the shell layer. Not as in shell suit but as in a waterproof and windproof shell. When you're active, it is important that the outer layer is breathable, otherwise the sweat you produce will end up making you wet and, ultimately, cold. Old-fashioned plastic cagoules are out (shame). Go for ventile cotton, a 100% natural material invented by boffins (yes, actual boffins) in World War Two to save the lives of pilots who had ditched in the sea. The fabric is warm, waterproof and in WWII it increased survival times in water from a few minutes to over 20. Enough time for a rescue. Enough said.

LEGS ELEVEN: With over-trousers, go for breathable fabrics or you'll start to sweat very quickly. Alternatively, go for breathable trousers that have waterproof qualities. At the very least avoid jeans. They stay wet for ages, get really heavy and can make your legs go blue.

HAPPY FEET: A sturdy waterproof walking boot might sound like a joke in the making, but think again. Goretex liners help your feet to breathe and will keep you dry. Leather and dubbin is a classic, tried-and-tested combo.

COSY TOES: Try alpaca socks (from www.jarbon.com) – they're warm in winter, cool in summer and don't make your feet sweat. Lovely.

Are you sleeping comfortably?

So you have your wardrobe sorted, but what about sleeping equipment? Choosing the perfect bag can present a world of mystery and it's uncomfortable when you get it wrong, even in the height of summer. The European Standard (EN13537) gives you the:

UPPER LIMIT OR MAXIMUM RATING. The highest temperature at which you can sleep comfortably without sweating (based on a standard man aged 25 with a height of 1.73m and a weight of 73kg).

COMFORT RATING. The temperature at which a standard woman (25-years-old, with a height of 1.60m and a weight of 60kg) can have a comfortable night's sleep.

LOWER LIMIT OR MINIMUM RATING. The lowest temperature at which the standard man can have a comfortable night's sleep.

EXTREME RATING. The point at which the standard woman will be protected from hypothermia.

OK that's cool, or warm, or hot, but what about with jim-jams? What if you're not standard? Skinny campers will feel the cold more. And whilst these ratings are given for the person with clothes on, they don't specify what kind of clothes. I'll assume it's a pair of long johns and a t-shirt. How romantic. Surely it's vest and undies all the way (including the girls)? I haven't worn pyjamas since I was seven and I'm not going to start again now. So I'm going to need an extra-warm sleeping bag.

Bag shape and style
The shape of your bag will also affect the kind of night's sleep you'll get. Generally:

MUMMY SHAPES will warm you up quicker and stay warm longer because there is less chance of colder air circulating. Some people (i.e. me) find the shape restrictive.

LOZENGE SHAPES will allow you to move around more freely whilst still retaining the body shape and some of the warming properties.

STANDARD/RECTANGULAR SHAPES will fulfil your needs but they aren't the warmest. On the plus side, you can zip a couple together to make a double bag. Handy for the marrieds and, I would argue, essential for romantic relations.

SLEEPING BAG LINERS will make your bag warmer and make it easier for you to keep clean as well as give you the option of sleeping in a cotton sheet.

Broader seasonal rating

This is used to show how you might use the bags in typical UK conditions:

ONE SEASON BAGS are for indoor use or for use in a hot climate.
TWO SEASON BAGS are for use from late spring to early autumn: temperatures above 9°C.
THREE SEASON BAGS can be used from early spring to late autumn: temperatures down to 0°C.
FOUR SEASON BAGS are for harsh conditions or for people who really feel the cold. They are designed for winter backpacking or climbing.

Translating that into van speak

Of course, your choice of bag will also depend on how well insulated your van is. If you've got all-night central heating (see page 244) then you may be able to get away with much less bedding as long as you don't mind using up precious gas supplies on very cold nights. Otherwise, consider thermal mats, which are available from Just Kampers (www.justkampers.com). They stick onto the interior of your windows and offer insulation against cold, not to mention extreme heat in summer (perish the thought).

Finally... have an awning practice run in the garden

I know you know how to put up your awning. I know you've been doing it for years. I know you know what you're doing. But really, honestly, can you tell me the last time you did it? If you have to think about it for more than 30 seconds I can recommend that you have a dry run, in the sunshine, before you set off. You simply don't know when you're going to arrive and what the conditions will be like when you get there. I can say this from experience. I recently put up my awning in the dark, when it was raining, having not put it up for over a year. A dry run might have been useful for that trip, yes. What a mess I made of it too.

To kick off our camper van year, here's something for you to bake to take. This is the stuff you… er… bake to take with you in a little Tupperware pot, stash in the cupboard and hope the kids don't find before you set off. If you were travelling north from Devon up the M5, for instance, I'd say that you'd need these around junction 7 or 8, just to keep things running smoothly. Get the picture? Don't scoff them all at once.

parmesan shortbreads,
WITH A SPICY KICK

How about a little savoury nibble for the road ahead? Go for it. These beauties freeze well so you can make them well ahead. If you like a mere hint of heat, use only a quarter of a teaspoon of cayenne, but if you like yours nicey spicey, don't hold back.

MAKES ABOUT 20
100G PLAIN FLOUR
75G PARMESAN, FINELY GRATED
75G COLD UNSALTED BUTTER, CUBED
1 LARGE EGG YOLK
¼-½ TSP CAYENNE PEPPER
SESAME SEEDS, TO SPRINKLE

Whiz all the ingredients, apart from the sesame seeds, together in a processor until they form a ball – this will take a few minutes.

Tip the dough onto a board and roll it into a sausage shape, about 22 cm in length. Wrap the dough in plastic wrap and chill it for 30 minutes (or longer is fine).

Preheat oven to 200°C/Fan 180°C/Gas 6. Slice the roll into 20 or so discs and transfer them to a large baking sheet. Sprinkle with sesame seeds if you fancy.

Bake for 12-15 minutes or until lightly golden. Carefully remove and cool on a wire rack.

lemon ginger squares

I like a bit of ginger. I like a bit of lemon too. So instead of arranging a fight, let's get them to work together. If you're feeling naughty, cut them into oblongs, not squares. They'll still taste delicious.

MAKES 16

200G GINGER NUT BISCUITS
75G BUTTER, MELTED
1 TBSP DEMERARA SUGAR

FOR THE TOPPING

2 LARGE EGGS
100G SOFT UNSALTED BUTTER
200G CASTER SUGAR
100G PLAIN FLOUR
JUICE OF 2-3 LEMONS (ABOUT 100MLS)

Whiz the biscuits to crumbs in a food processor (or crush in a freezer bag using a rolling pin). Melt the 75g of butter, then mix with the biscuit crumbs and the demerara sugar and tip into an 18 cm square tin, ideally loose-bottomed. Chill the base while you make the topping and preheat the oven to 180°C/Fan 160°C/Gas 4.

Lightly beat the eggs in a bowl. Next, in a mixer, beat together the butter and sugar until combined, then gradually add the eggs. Sift in the flour and add the lemon juice too. Mix to combine.

Tip the lemon mixture onto the biscuit base and bake for 30-35 minutes or until set and golden at the edges. Leave to cool in the tin before cutting into squares.

chocolate hokey pokey bites

Chocolate! You love it. But not too much or you'll never get off the driveway. These will keep for days in a Tupperware box or tin so you know, save them. Each one will give you a satisfying sweet nugget of crunchiness. Just what the doctor never would have ordered.

MAKES ABOUT 28

75G UNSALTED BUTTER

100G PECAN HALVES, ROUGHLY CHOPPED

SEA SALT FLAKES

300G DARK CHOCOLATE

2 TBSP GOLDEN SYRUP

3 X 40G CRUNCHIE BARS

Heat a small knob of the butter in a pan and when foaming, tip in the pecans with a pinch of crushed sea salt flakes, stir over a medium heat for 3-4 minutes or till toasted – you will smell them when they are ready. Tip the toasted nuts into a bowl and leave to cool.

Break the chocolate into pieces and melt, in a medium pan, with the rest of the butter and the syrup, stirring. Once the chocolate mixture is smooth take the pan off the heat. Chop the Crunchie bars, then add the chunks, along with the toasted pecans, to the chocolate mixture. Gently mix together before transferring to an 18 cm round or square cake tin. Leave to set – a couple of hours at room temperature or about an hour in the fridge.

Remove the chocolate 'cake' from the tin and cut into quarters, then cut each quarter into 7 or 8 angular chunks.

raspberry and banana traybake
WITH CINNAMON CRUMBLE TOPPING

If you're heading off, this could be your last option to use your whisk and oven and make a proper baking-type mess before you return to your fully formed kitchen. So why not make something really special? This is it.

MAKES 24 SQUARES

225G SOFT BUTTER

4 LARGE EGGS

200G LIGHT MUSCOVADO SUGAR

150G SELF-RAISING FLOUR

50G GROUND ALMONDS

1 ROUNDED TSP BAKING POWDER

3 MEDIUM, VERY RIPE BANANAS,
  PEELED AND MASHED

175G RASPBERRIES

FOR THE CRUMBLE TOPPING

75G DEMERARA SUGAR

75G COLD UNSALTED BUTTER, CUBED

100G SELF-RAISING FLOUR

2 TSP GROUND CINNAMON

100G UNBLANCHED ALMONDS

FOR THE LEMON DRIZZLE

100G ICING SUGAR

JUICE OF HALF A LEMON

Preheat the oven to 180°C/Fan 160°C/Gas 4.

In a mixer, whisk together the butter, eggs, sugar, flour, ground almonds and baking powder until smooth and combined.

Peel and mash the bananas and fold them into the mixture, then tip the whole lot into a lined 20 x 33cm base x 3-4 cm deep tin. Spread the mixture out and smooth over the surface. Scatter the raspberries on top.

For the crumble topping, in a food processor, whiz together the sugar, butter, flour and cinnamon until they form crumbs, then add the nuts and whiz again until chopped. Finally add 2 dessertspoons of water and give the crumble one final whiz until it forms small clumps (or, rub the ingredients together to crumbs by hand, then chop the nuts and add with the water before mixing). Sprinkle the crumble topping over the raspberries.

Bake the traybake for 45-50 minutes or until risen and golden all over. Leave to cool completely in the tin.

For the lemon drizzle, sift the icing sugar into a bowl and gradually add enough lemon juice to make a thick icing, mixing until smooth. Drizzle over the top of the crumble, leave to set. Cut into squares.

TAKE IT WITH YOU — THERMOS FLASK COOKERY

A little while ago I met a very nice lady on my travels called Elizabeth. During the conversation she mentioned something about cooking in a Thermos flask. A couple of days later it struck me what a genius idea this was. Apparently, the method was developed during times of austerity (proper austerity that is, not our soft, modern austerity) when electricity cuts were common, fuel was expensive and households had smaller disposable incomes than they have today. The idea is to start cooking on the stove, then transfer your food to a Thermos so that it can slow cook for the rest of the day. Clever. And it's very simple.

⋆ Fill your Thermos with boiling water and secure the lid (a wide-mouthed one is best).
⋆ Begin the cooking process at home for your stew, or in this case rice pudding, before you leave.
⋆ Empty the flask and pour the part-cooked rice pudding into the warm Thermos flask (a funnel is handy). Set off on your journey.
⋆ When you get there, several hours later, you eat.

thermos RICE PUDDING

◀ FOR 2

SMALL KNOB BUTTER
3 LEVEL TBSP (50G) SHORT GRAIN PUDDING RICE
650MLS WHOLE MILK
1 TBSP CASTER SUGAR
¼ TSP GROUND CINNAMON
A DOLLOP OF JAM, TO SERVE

Fill your Thermos with boiling water and set aside.

Put all the ingredients for the pud into a pan. Bring to the boil then reduce the heat and simmer very gently over a low heat for 15 minutes, giving it a stir from time to time – keep an eye on the pan as the milk boils over easily.

Empty the flask and pour the hot rice pudding into it, screw on the lid and set off on your big adventure. After 3½-4 hours, eat with a dollop of jam.

Time for a brew

Now then. Anyone who knows me will know that I can't function without a decent cup of tea. I've probably made more cups of tea in my short and sweet forty-something years than the average person will do in a lifetime. Which is why our kettle is a carefully chosen and highly valued piece of camper van equipment. Access to the cupboard where it resides must never be compromised. Just in case you get an invite for the night, you know.

APPRECIATING A FINE CUP OF TEA

The Tea Appreciation Society care about tea and know an awful lot more about it than me. You'll find their four seasonal ideas for making best use of that happy whistling kettle in the seasonal chapters of this book. If the suggestions sound a bit posh, don't panic, it's just tea. And it's blooming lovely.

SPRING

Today is a good day to go camping

Spring is a good time to start the camper van year because it's full of hope. It's a time for looking forward. Summer and all its carefree promise is just around the corner. As soon as the daffs open up their cheerful bonnets, we can start to feel like it's beginning to happen at last.

The middle of March is also the time when British Summer Time begins, officially. After the long nights of winter the days begin to lengthen. The sun wakes up again and feels warm on your back. That alone should serve to jolly us up a bit. OK so the mornings might begin with a crunch on frosty grass, but by lunchtime you'll find yourself stripped down to your vest and undies and thinking of taking a swim.

Spring is full of special days and celebrations, which, in turn, bring food and adventures. It also has three out of four of our national days: St David's, St Patrick's and St George's. And don't forget St Piran's Day.

Shrove Tuesday is the day to mix up a pancake or two in preparation for the fasting of Lent. If you've given up anything then you'll be pleased to know that it's just 40 days and nights until Easter. But, of course, if you are Irish and have given up stout you can always claim your get out of jail free card and get the 'day off' on 17th March. It's OK, apparently.

After your days and nights of fasting, you'll be chomping at the bit for a bit of R-and-R at Easter. This is when the rest of the nation wakes up suddenly and heads for the coast with a musty tent and a leaky blow-up mattress for an ice cream and a bag of chips. Not you. You'll be cosy in the van with a plateful of mussels in white wine and cream (see page 47).

Oh yes. And it's National SPAM Appreciation week in early March. You don't have to go if you don't want to. There will be plenty of other things to be getting on with. But if you want a nostalgic taste of times gone by, then the time is right. Fry up a spam hash for brekkie, why don't you? Maybe not.

Get out there!

The first day of Spring

OK, here we go. Spring has officially sprung. It's that special day when you wake up and look out of the window and think to yourself, 'today is a good day to go camping'. And, as long as you've done your prep, you should be ready to hit the road in search of more coastal camper van capers. Days are longer, frosts are less of a problem and the evenings are getting lighter all the time. The sea is still a bit parky and the nights can be tepid at best, but what the hell? It's time to fire up the van and hit the road again.

Ten signs of spring

★ The clocks go forward
★ The daffodils come out
★ Wild garlic shoots up in the woods
★ Pigeons start giving each other piggy backs
★ The papers start writing about the Great British Picnic
★ The price of VW vans goes up
★ You can't find your flip flops
★ Suddenly there are lots of Bank Holidays
★ You can't wait to get out there and get camping
★ If you surf you can take off your hood and gloves, at last

WHAT'S ON THE STEREO?

I have developed a new theory about music.

The idea is that at least one CD in your collection (or playlist if you're talking digital) should be devoted to the year in which your van came out of the factory. So when you take it out it will be able to hear what could have been playing on the factory radio when it was put together (I like to imagine). Nineteen seventy-nine was the year that my current van was built. Happily it was a good year for music. Some say it was the last good year for music. How about your van? If you've got a late Splitty then you're in for a summer of love from '67 every time you step on the gas, and if you're lucky enough to own one of the handful of the very first Westfalias still in existence from 1951 then you're in for a treat, but you'd better pack your cardigan. It's Perry Como and Doris Day for you. How about your 1990 T4? Inspiral Carpets, Soup Dragons and Primal Scream will be rocking your world.

But, for now, back to 1979. Here's what's on the stereo:

Reasons to be Cheerful Part 3 – IAN DURY AND THE BLOCKHEADS
Transmission – JOY DIVISION • Union City Blue – BLONDIE
Up the Junction – SQUEEZE • Into the Valley – SKIDS
Get Over You – THE UNDERTONES • **Stop Your Sobbing – THE PRETENDERS**
Pop Muzik – M • Baby I Love You – THE RAMONES
Breakfast in America – SUPERTRAMP

See, I told you. Good isn't it?

Cast off those winter plumes

The first swim of the year

So the sap is rising and you're feeling invincible? And doesn't that sea look inviting, what with all the sparkling sunlight dancing upon it and everything?

Taking your very first dip of the year can be a memorable experience. Somehow, getting on, in or under the water (hopefully all three) after a long hot drive is extraordinarily cathartic. Think of the sucking of breath as the water reaches your thighs and the tightening of your skin as your stomach flees the slap of the chop. Think of tippy toes in the sand, keeping you just that little bit drier before you take the plunge and dive in. And then think of the ooohs and the aaaahs and it's not that bad, come-on-ins as you take a few dizzy strokes. Great stuff.

The Victorians knew that outdoor swimming was good for us and thankfully we're rediscovering it, one beach, lake, river and loch at a time. Kate Rew, founder of the Outdoor Swimming Society (www.outdoorswimmingsociety.com), has been swimming in the wild since childhood and has made it part of her life's work to bring us closer to the water. Her book, *Wild Swim*, is full of marvellous places to take a dip. Some, like the blue lagoon in Pembrokeshire, are truly inspiring and enough to make me want to pack up the van right now and go there.

At this time of the year, the water is at its coldest, since the sea takes so long to heat up and cool down, so whilst land temperatures might be hitting the mid teens, sea temperatures are going to be well below double figures until May or June. Effectively, you could well experience colder sea temperatures in April than you'd expect to find in December at the Boxing Day dip. But if you are up for the challenge, do yourself a favour and check out the guidelines for swimming in cold water (page 283). The secret, so they tell me, is to breathe out as you hit the water.

Spring tides, hidden treasures

Spring tides are especially strong tides (rising highest and falling lowest) that occur during a full or new moon, at any time of the year. When the earth, the sun and the moon are in a line, the gravitational forces are at their strongest. The 'spring' refers to the tide springing up, rather than anything to do with the season. That said, around the vernal equinox (21st March), the spring tides are the biggest of the year.

Beachcombing is rewarding on any day, but with big spring tides you'll get to see parts of the beach that are rarely visible. At low tide, the lower foreshore will be exposed, meaning you are more likely to see busy rock pools, pick the biggest mussels and have access to anemones, worms and seaweeds that would otherwise be hiding underwater. Spring tides move quicker than at other times and they can catch fish and shellfish out. So watch out for starfish, crabs, prawns and shrimp. And if you poke about in holes with a gaff for long enough, lobster and crabs. You might even find the elusive razor clam or some edible seaweeds. Happy hunting.

On low spring tides, look out for

★ Ancient wreckage and the skeletons of old boats in the sand.

★ Caves, beaches and rock arches that are normally inaccessible.

★ Kelps and seaweeds that are usually covered.

★ Rock pools that rarely get uncovered.

★ Ancient tree stumps (at Porlock, Westward Ho!, Borth Beach in West Wales and more).

★ Flotsam (goods lost from a ship that has sunk or otherwise perished) and jetsam (goods cast overboard to lighten a vessel that is in danger of sinking).

★ Bottles with messages. And if you find one with a phone number in it, ring it and tell them off for littering. Don't offer any kind of rescue service.

Finally

Watch out for the tide. As fast as it goes out it will come in again. So keep an eye on your exit and make sure you are always able to get back. If you are going somewhere remote, make sure someone knows where you are, charge up your mobile phone (although you won't get a signal everywhere) and wear sensible footwear. Also, go as the tide drops, know when it's low and make a move before it comes back in.

clams with
CHORIZO AND SHERRY

Like cockles, clams live in the sand and can be foraged at low water with a rake or a spade. Not to be confused with razor clams, which are much more difficult to get hold of. If you have no joy, put a call in to the fishmonger.

FOR 2
KNOB OF BUTTER
OLIVE OIL
2 SHALLOTS (OR 1 SMALL ONION), FINELY CHOPPED
2 TBSP CHORIZO (OR BACON), FINELY CHOPPED
A SHORT TUMBLERFUL (200MLS) MANZANILLA OR FINO SHERRY
6 GENEROUS HANDFULS (1KG) CLAMS, CLEANED
PARSLEY, CHOPPED
BREAD, TO SERVE

Melt the butter with a tablespoon of oil in a large pan and gently cook the shallots for 3-4 minutes. Stir in the chorizo and fry together for 3-4 minutes more.

Pour the sherry into the pan and bring to simmering point. Bubble the liquid for a minute, then tip in the clams and once everything is bubbling again, clamp on a tight-fitting lid. Cook the clams over a high heat for 6-8 minutes or until they have opened (discard any that don't). Avoid adding seasoning as the clams are likely to be salty themselves.

Scatter the parsley into the pan, then transfer the clams and the delicious broth into two bowls. Add an extra drizzle of olive oil to each. Eat with bread.

MUSSELS in WHITE WINE
and cream with WILD GARLIC

Mussels are my favourite food. This is because you can cook them in one pot and they taste great however you do them. They also come in their own biodegradable packaging that you can simply leave on the beach when you go. Also, if you dare to pick them yourself, you can guarantee low food miles and the very freshest ingredients you could ever hope for.

◀ FOR 2

50G BUTTER

1 SMALL ONION, FINELY CHOPPED

HALF GLASS OF WHITE WINE

JUICE AND ZEST OF A LEMON

10 LEAVES OF WILD GARLIC (OR A FEW CLOVES OF NORMAL GARLIC), FINELY CHOPPED

2KG MUSSELS, SCRUBBED AND BEARDS REMOVED

A BIG GLUG (100MLS) OF SINGLE CREAM

SMALL BUNCH OF PARSLEY, FINELY CHOPPED

CRUSTY BREAD, TO SERVE

In a large pan, melt the butter, then add the onion and gently fry for 7-8 minutes. Add the wine and bubble away for a few minutes, to allow the alcohol to evaporate, before adding the juice and zest of the lemon (and chopped garlic cloves, if you can't find the wild stuff).

Once everything is bubbling away nicely, tip in the mussels and clamp on the lid. Steam for about 5 minutes over a medium-high heat until most of the mussels have opened (discard any that don't) – give them a shake from time to time as they cook.

Just before serving add the cream, wild garlic and parsley. Stir together and serve with some fresh crusty bread, as is fitting with food this easy and tasty.

crab, watercress, tomato
AND NEW POTATO HASH

If you can't get watercress then try this with a bunch of chopped chives. Just as tasty.

FOR 2
9 OR 10 MEDIUM-SIZED NEW POTATOES (500G)
2 ONIONS
BUTTER AND OLIVE OIL, FOR FRYING
2 MEDIUM TOMATOES
ZEST OF A LEMON
1 RED CHILLI, IF YOU FANCY IT
2 OR 3 HANDFULS WATERCRESS
MEAT FROM A MEDIUM-SIZED DRESSED CRAB (OR 200G MIXED CRABMEAT)
SEA SALT FLAKES

Boil the potatoes in salted water for 10-15 minutes or until tender. Drain and cool before halving or cutting into chunks. Meanwhile, peel and chop the onions. Heat the butter and a tablespoon of oil in a frying pan and when foaming, tip in the onions – cook for 10-15 minutes or until softened. Meanwhile, chop the tomatoes, then halve, deseed and finely chop the chili, if using. Roughly chop the watercress.

When the onions are ready, tip them into a bowl and add the tomatoes, lemon zest, chilli, watercress and crabmeat. Toss together.

Add another slug of oil to the frying pan and fry the potatoes over a high heat until golden. Tip in all the other ingredients and toss everything together over the heat until hot and sizzling, adding salt to taste. Eat straight from the pan or pile onto two plates.

Go Seaweed foraging

I am fascinated by seaweed. Whilst other cultures celebrate it as a delicious and versatile ingredient, its culinary virtues are something that we have either forgotten or chosen to ignore, even though our entire country is surrounded by the stuff and none of our seaweeds are poisonous. Spring is a good time to go looking for seaweed, as you'll be able to clearly see the difference between the new spring growth and last year's growth.

My friend Fraser Christian, a professional forager, took me on a seaweed ramble along a remote part of the Jurassic Coast near Burton Bradstock to see what had been revealed by the March spring tides. We talked seaweed, as you do. We ate it too. If you have the chance, book a day with someone like Fraser (try www. coastalsurvival.com). You'll find out lots of interesting things. Such as:

THE INTERTIDAL ZONE is the area between the highest and lowest spring tides. This can be divided roughly into three sections by the colour of the seaweed that grows there (although, of course, with nature being nature, the zones overlap).

THE GREEN ZONE is the part nearest the high tide mark. Here you are likely to find green seaweeds like gut weed and sea lettuce. Both are edible, although gut weed likes brackish water so can often be found in or near streams and rivers (so exercise caution).

Gut weed can be stir-fried. Try it with a little leftover potato and corned beef. Gut weed hash! It can also be used as a natural cap to put on top of limpets so they steam in their own juices (that's Fraser's idea). Dried it's a little like the deep fried cabbage that doubles as seaweed in Chinese restaurants.

Sea lettuce is one of the few seaweeds that is very palatable raw. It looks like a very delicate lettuce leaf. In *Food For Free*, Richard Mabey recommends eating it with soy sauce as part of a salad. I like eating it when walking along the beach with friends. They find it a bit freaky. It's best when picked from sand-free rock pools.

THE RED ZONE is the middle part of the foreshore where, on the whole, the red coloured seaweeds grow. This includes dulse, an old favourite that can be eaten raw. It begins to re-grow in the spring when it will be beautifully translucent when held up to the light. Avoid eating it when it is tatty or has other organisms growing on it.

Dulse can be eaten raw or dried and eaten as a snack. It has long been eaten on the west coast of Ireland where it grows well in the clear waters of the Atlantic. It can also be found around the UK coast. Pepper Dulse is of the same family but has smaller fronds and grows closer to the rocks. It has, as the name suggests, a peppery taste.

Purple Laver is the one seaweed that still gets eaten in the UK (it is used for making the traditional laverbread in Wales). It is very thin when it grows but still needs to be boiled in water for at least four hours before it can be used. Once it has formed a broken mass, roll it in oats and form into small patties. Then fry it in bacon fat and serve with poached eggs and bacon.

Carrageen Moss is another reddish seaweed that has long been used in puddings and recipes because it contains natural agar, a thickening agent. It can be boiled to extract the agar. This can then be used to thicken drinks or puddings. Added to milk with cinnamon or vanilla, it makes a blancmange-like pudding that's surprisingly delicious. See my recipe on page 53.

THE BROWN ZONE is the lowest part of the intertidal zone and can only be accessed during spring tides. This is where you will find the kelps. Sugar kelp is one such kelp that's easy to recognise and pick. Once dried it can be eaten like a snack and has a crisp-like quality with a sweet taste.

The small print

Seaweed clings onto the rocks with clasps, so if you pull and tear it off, you will kill it. For a sustainable harvest, use a knife to cut the seaweed, leaving a part of the frond (about a third) and all of the clasp intact. That way it can begin to grow again.

Seaweed is vegetable matter and will rot once it separates from the rocks. Don't eat seaweed that you find at the high tide mark.

The quality of seaweed will depend on the quality of the water in which it lives. As with all seafood, make sure you know how good the water quality is before you go picking. If there is the slightest risk of pollution, leave well alone.

Most seaweed is edible and none is poisonous, but you should still take your time and identify first, then think about picking.

Collect sustainably – that means collecting from a wide area, not disturbing other wildlife and not taking more than you need.

As with all foraging, seaweed picking is governed by the rules of ownership and conservation objectives, no matter where it grows. So please, seek permission from the landowner first and pick responsibly for your own use only.

sugar kelp crisps
CAMPER VAN STYLE

◄ The dashboard of your van is a good place to dry seaweed. With the dashboard in direct sunlight, a piece of sugar kelp will dry in no time (turning bright green as it begins to dry out). So... find yourself one long strand of sugar kelp. Cut it with a sharp knife about 10 cm in from the rocks, leaving a few centimetres of frond so it will re-grow. Place it on a sunny dashboard for 2-3 hours or until crispy. Then break into small pieces and eat like crisps.

martin's SEA MOSS

A traditional Caribbean drink, this beautiful, milky cocktail is made thick by the natural agar in the carrageen moss. Supposedly it's got aphrodisiac properties. I can't say for sure, but when I discovered that I could make it in my van with seaweed that I'd picked off the shore, I got very excited indeed. But not in that way... You can buy carrageen moss or pick it from the shore. Just make sure it's free from rot and parasites.

◄ MAKES 6-8 SERVINGS
HANDFUL FRESH CARRAGEEN MOSS
CINNAMON STICK
1 LITRE MILK
2 TBSP DEMERARA SUGAR, OR MORE ACCORDING TO TASTE
½ TSP GROUND NUTMEG
DARK RUM, ICE AND A SPRIG OF CARRAGEEN, TO SERVE

Rinse the carrageen moss in fresh water. Add it, along with 300mls of water and the cinnamon stick to a saucepan and bring to the boil. Simmer for 20 minutes. Next, strain the mixture and return the gelatine-like liquid to the pan (discarding the cinnamon and moss), along with the milk, sugar and nutmeg. Re-boil and simmer for another 10 minutes. Taste and, if you like it sweeter, add more sugar. Allow to cool, then, if necessary, whisk to mix. Serve in glasses with rum and ice and a sprig of carrageen as a garnish.

Visit a seaweed bath

Seaweed isn't just for slipping on or nibbling tentatively, it's remarkable stuff that contains all kinds of good-for-you minerals – used in everything from beauty products to wound-packing materials. The seaweed spa came about because farmers on the west coast of Ireland, who handled seaweed to fertilise the fields, noticed that cuts and calluses on their hands healed well. Some bright spark put two and two together and invented the bath.

If you've never experienced one, I can suggest you pack up the van and get a ferry to Ireland straight away. And if you live in Ireland then I suggest you… you know the score. If you want to, you can even take a friend with you and enjoy double the fun.

Seaweed baths are located at:

BUNDORAN, County Donegal info@waterworldbundoran.com
STRANDHILL, County Donegal www.voyaseaweedbaths.com
NEWCASTLE, County Down www.soakseaweedbaths.co.uk
BALLYBUNION, County Kerry tel: +353 068 27469
ENNISCRONE, County Sligo www.kilcullenseaweedbaths.com

Make your own seaweed bath

This might not be as easy as going to a seaweed bath, as you've more than likely forgotten to pack a bath. But a big washing-up bowl full of hot seawater and a few strands of Fucus Serratus (toothed wrack) will enable you to experience a little of the silky smooth feeling a hot seaweed bath will give you.

Wait until you get a really warm late spring day.

★ Collect some seaweed from the beach below the high tide mark. Cut it about a third of the way down the stem rather than pull it straight from the rock. Don't be tempted to use dead seaweed.

☆ Fill up a big pan with fresh clean seawater and heat it over the stove but don't boil it. When it's hot, pour it over the seaweed in your washing-up bowl or bucket. Repeat until your washing-up bowl is full.

★ Now strip off and rub the seaweed all over your body. If that feels wrong, simply wash in the brown-coloured water that the seaweed makes. It will feel smooth and silky.

☆ Once you've scrubbed, dash into the sea to clean off the seaweed water. Or better still, get someone to lob a cold bucket of seawater over or at you.

Whilst you can buy most ingredients in the supermarket, there are some things that you'll only get on a walk along the beach or in the country, such as wild garlic and sea beet. If you've never tried them, do, because their taste is unique. Naturally you'll need to be 100% sure it is what it is before you eat, but those that I've chosen are easy to identify and hard to mistake.

scrambled eggs
WITH WILD GARLIC

How better to kick off the springtime, than with a favourite breakfast (or anytime snack) of scrambled eggs with wild garlic? It's not rocket science but it is delicious. If there's one bit of foraging you do this spring, make sure it's wild garlic you go for. You'll smell it before you see it.

MAKES A HEARTY BREAKFAST FOR 1, A HAPPY SNACK FOR 2

3 LARGE EGGS
2 TBSP MILK
2 SLICES BREAD
KNOB OF BUTTER, PLUS EXTRA FOR THE TOAST
DASH OF CREAM, IF YOU ARE FEELING DECADENT
1-2 TBSP WILD GARLIC LEAVES, CHOPPED

Preheat the grill.

Whisk the eggs and milk together, in a bowl, with some seasoning. Toast the bread on both sides, then butter and keep warm.

Heat the knob of butter in a pan and when foaming, tip in the eggs. Stir over a medium heat for a minute or until there is only a little liquid egg remaining. Take the pan off the heat and stir in the cream, if using, and the wild garlic. Spoon onto the hot buttered toast.

Poached eggs with
BLACK PUDDING AND SEA BEET

This breakfast is eggs Florentine, coastal-style, but without the hollandaise sauce. Eggs go perfectly with sea beet, which is very similar to spinach (it's also known as sea spinach). The black pudding adds a little extra something, although you can always do without.

◀ FOR 2
GENEROUS HANDFUL SEA BEET (OR SPINACH), SHREDDED
4-6 SLICES BLACK PUDDING
4 VERY FRESH LARGE EGGS
2 MUFFINS, SPLIT
BUTTER, FOR SPREADING
MAYONNAISE, TO SERVE

There are a lot of ways of getting poached eggs 'perfect'. Some use a special pan whilst others use vinegar to keep the whole thing together. Not me. I prefer the vortex approach. It's simple: get your pan of water boiling and then get a spoon and whip the water into a vortex with circular movements. Next, quickly crack your eggs into the middle of the vortex.

Preheat the grill on a high setting and bring a pan of water to the boil – put the sea beet in a sieve over the pan of water and cover. Get your black pudding under the grill and cooking as soon as the grill is hot. Once the water has boiled and the black pudding is almost done, get that vortex going and crack the eggs into the water – place the sieve containing the sea beet back over the pan and cover so it continues to steam whilst the eggs cook. Toast the muffins and butter them. After two minutes, haul the eggs out with a slotted spoon and pat them dry with kitchen roll. Leave the sea beet over the water if it is not yet cooked to your liking, then season when it is ready. Serve the eggs on the toasted muffins with the sea beet, in a big pile, and add a little dollop of mayonnaise on the side.

WILD GARLIC pesto

A firm favourite in the van. Using half basil and half wild garlic leaves, and omitting the usual garlic cloves, will transform your standard recipe. Some people even use just wild garlic. That is up to you and your tastes. This is simplicity itself and, of course (if you ask me), it tastes better than any shop-bought pesto. Even the kids will eat it. Spoon it into a bowl of hot penne, sprinkle with extra parmesan and finish with a wild garlic flower. Bellissimo!

◀ FOR 2, GENEROUSLY
9 TBSP PINE NUTS
LARGE BUNCH OF BASIL, FINELY CHOPPED
BUNCH OF WILD GARLIC LEAVES, FINELY CHOPPED
ABOUT 8 TBSP OLIVE OIL
8 TBSP FINELY GRATED PARMESAN

Crush the pine nuts in a pestle and mortar. Add the basil and wild garlic leaves and crush together. Add half the olive oil, a little at a time. Stir in the parmesan and season. Add the remaining oil and mix together.

nettle soup with CRISPY BACON

If there's one thing you'll find when you're out and about in your van, it's stingers. So why not freak out your family and try my stinging nettle soup. It's relatively easy to make in the van without an electric whizzer and it's delicious, so worth the hassle.

◀ FOR 4

OIL FOR FRYING
4 RASHERS SMOKED BACON, CHOPPED SMALL
1 MEDIUM RED ONION, FINELY CHOPPED
4 SMALLISH POTATOES (450G), PEELED AND CUBED
1 CLOVE GARLIC, FINELY CHOPPED
2 GENEROUS DOUBLE HANDFULS YOUNG NETTLE LEAVES (WEAR GLOVES),
   STEMS REMOVED
800MLS VEGETABLE (OR CHICKEN) STOCK
2-3 TBSP DOUBLE CREAM

Add a dash of oil to a saucepan. Fry the bacon until crispy, then scoop out and set aside.

Add the onion and potatoes to the pan. Cook over a medium heat until the onions are soft and the potato is almost cooked. Stir in the garlic and fry for a further few minutes.

Meanwhile, chop the nettles as small as you can get them – use gloves (they only lose their sting once they are cooked). Add the nettles to the pan, along with the stock. Slowly bring the liquid to the boil, simmer, partially covered, for 10 minutes. Take the pan off the heat and mash the soup with a potato masher. Then strain the soup through a sieve into a bowl, mashing the pulp with the back of a spoon as you do so. Discard any larger leaves that won't fit through the sieve. Season generously.

Ladle into bowls. Stir a little cream into each one and sprinkle crispy bacon on top.

The shipping forecast

Tyne, Dogger, German Bight. During the eighties, when I started surfing there was no internet or wifi or smartphones to give you your surf and weather reports. To find out what was happening you had to rely on the BBC weather map and the shipping forecast. I can still remember sitting in my old surfing friend Spout's van, huddled around the radio (it wasn't quite a crystal set but not far off) listening to the duty voice of BBC Radio 4, reading the forecast slowly and carefully. This is so that it's easy to write down, in case you were wondering.

In those days, the shipping forecast meant everything and we learnt to understand its complexities (or at least relied on Spout to translate it for us) to determine what kind of surf we could look forward to in the morning. Spout, always the die-hard, still listens to it.

Here's how it works

The shipping forecast uses a predetermined set of terms (set by the Met Office) to describe everything from the speed at which a pressure system is moving, to the sea state and the rate at which the atmospheric pressure is changing. Clarity and brevity are key, so whilst it might sound like gobbledegook at first, once you can begin to understand the terms, you will be able to unravel the wonders and the mysteries within.

★ The waters around the British Isles are divided into 31 sea areas shown on the map. Each forecast contains details of gale warnings in force, a general synopsis and sea-area forecasts containing forecast wind direction and force, rain (if any), sea state and visibility.

★ **The forecast usually starts at Viking, in the North Sea and works its way clockwise around the British Isles.**

★ The shipping forecast is issued four times a day by the Met Office at 23:00, 05:00, 11:00 and 17:00 GMT. Each forecast covers the following 24 hours.

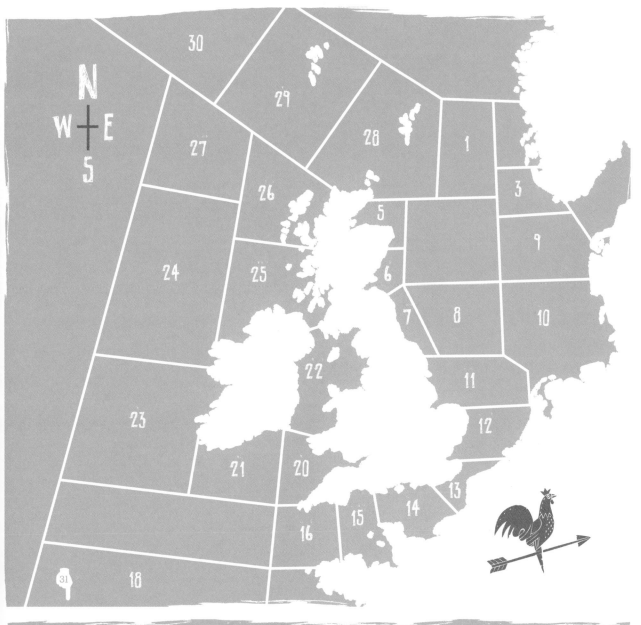

1. VIKING
2. N. UTSIRE
3. S. UTSIRE
4. FORTIES
5. CROMARTY
6. FORTH
7. TYNE
8. DOGGER
9. FISHER
10. GERMAN BIGHT
11. HUMBER
12. THAMES
13. DOVER
14. WIGHT
15. PORTLAND
16. PLYMOUTH
17. BISCAY
18. FITZROY
19. SOLE
20. LUNDY
21. FASTNET
22. IRISH SEA
23. SHANNON
24. ROCKALL
25. MALIN
26. HEBRIDES
27. BAILEY
28. FAIR ISLE
29. FAEROES
30. S.E. ICELAND
31. TRAFALGAR

★ Wind direction: The terms 'veering' and 'backing' refer to changes in wind direction. Veering indicates that the wind is changing in a clockwise direction whereas backing is in an anti-clockwise direction. 'Variable' means winds of less than force 4 that change by more than 90 degrees in the time or area. 'Cyclonic' means there will be considerable change.

★ Winds are described in the Beaufort scale, where 0 is no wind and 12 is hurricane force. As the wind gets stronger the scale uses terms to describe the wind strength. Three is a gentle breeze (between 9 and 12 mph), eight is a gale (between 39 and 46 mph) and 12 is hurricane force (above 73 mph).

★ Time is referred to in very precise terms. 'Then' means one kind of weather followed by another. 'Occasional' means something happening more than once but not for more than half of the forecast period. 'For a time' means a condition that happens once but not for more than half the period. 'At first' means a condition that happens at the beginning of the forecast that then changes. 'Later' means starting more than halfway through the forecast. 'Imminent' means within 6 hours and 'soon' means between 6 and 12 hours.

★ Visibility is exactly that: how far you can see. 'Good' means that visibility is greater than 5 nautical miles (or 5.8 mi). 'Moderate' is where visibility is between 2 and 5 nautical miles (2.3 and 5.8 mi). 'Poor' puts visibility at between 1,000 metres and 2 nautical miles.

★ Sea state can be described as anything from 'smooth', which means waves of less than half a metre, to 'phenomenal', which means waves of more than 14 metres.

★ Pressure can be described as 'rising' or 'falling', rising or falling slowly or rising or falling quickly. This is the speed at which the pressure is changing.

★ Pressure systems move at speeds that are described as 'slowly' (moving at less than 15 knots), 'steadily' (moving at 15 to 25 knots), 'rather quickly' (moving at 25 to 35 knots), 'rapidly' (moving at 35 to 45 knots), 'very rapidly' (moving at more than 45 knots).

Find out more at www.metoffice.gov.uk

SEASIDE SECRETS: The shipping forecast is never more than 370 words long.

Bank holidays

Spring is the season for bank holidays in the UK, which means that it's the season for getting away from it all. For many, the holiday weekends are an excuse to take a few days off and dash to the coast. So you'll expect to see jams, tents that haven't been up for a while, caravans with their wheels fallen off and lots of ill-prepared people who have forgotten what it's like to camp and have left everything at home that's useful. Alternatively, at the other end of the spectrum, you'll see those who have prepared too well and have brought everything with them, including the kitchen sink.

You, my camping friends, will be somewhere in the middle. I hope.

Bank holidays are the time to do what makes us British. We brave the weather, go for strolls, eat ice cream, consume chips on the seafront and get attacked by seagulls. We tackle deck chairs, put up wind breaks and pretend that everything is OK, even though it most probably isn't. And that's what makes British bank holidays such perfect times for people-watching.

People-watching

A fine Victorian idea that stands us in good stead today. It's what promenades were made for. You have a little walk, check out the other people and have a gossip about them. Just be careful how you do it. People don't like it if you stare at them. Especially if you look like a slackjaw.

ROCK AND PADSTOW, Cornwall. Perfect posh perusing. Watch for: big cars reversing ski boats, debutantes, shorts over wetsuits and rugby shirts with their collars up.

SIDMOUTH, Devon. Watch for: well-to-do oldies on the lovely Georgian seafront, and mobility scooters. Snoozing in deckchairs is a local speciality.

SANDBANKS, Dorset. Watch for: footballers and the mega rich. Don't confuse people-watching with perving at the nudist beach nearby.

BRIGHTON BEACH, East Sussex. Watch for: cool ex-London exiles, quirky bohemians, would-be surfer dudes and golden oldies. People-watching's finest. With glee.

BLACKPOOL, Lancashire. Watch for: good old-fashioned, salt of the earth, diamonds in the rough, kiss-me-quick, squeeze-me-slow people of all creeds and colours. There is nowhere else like it.

ABERSOCH, Llyn Peninsula. Watch for: yummy mummys, yachtie types, surfer dudes and wannabe wags. Fake tan by the bucket load.

WELLS-NEXT-THE-SEA, Norfolk. Watch for: all kinds including fishing-smock-wearing artists, jumbo-cord-wearing dads and Boden mummies. And some salty-dog fishermen for good measure.

WHITBY, Yorkshire. Watch for: frights, horrors and amazing costumes at Goth weekends in April and October.

It takes all sorts

Shrove Tuesday

Shrove Tuesday. Pancake Day. The last day before Lent. Your chance to indulge before it's all over for 40 days and 40 nights. You feast, then you fast. It's good, every once in a while, to abstain and have a little think whilst you do it. Because that's what it's all about.

One of the nicest Shrove Tuesday rituals I've seen is - handily near me in Devon - at the oh-so-cutesy seaside village of Clovelly. It's called Lansherd and it involves all the children of the village racing through the cobbled streets trailing tin cans on lengths of string. The noise is designed to drive the devil into the sea. Some of the residents told me that it used to be a big deal in the village, with biscuit tins, kettles and cans – and even an old tin bath – being used to scare the devil away. Finally, when everyone gets to the harbour, the tin cans are chucked into the sea (don't worry, they collect them in the morning).

Lansherd is a lovely thing to see and it's even better to know that, as the kids rattle off down the steep and narrow cobbled streets, one of our weird and wonderful British seaside traditions is being kept alive. Bring string, an old tin bath and meet me by the fountain at six and I'll show you (www.clovelly.co.uk).

Alternatively, get yourself over to Scarborough, North Yorkshire and celebrate with the town's annual skipping festival. Listen out for the pancake bell ...

PANCAKES

◀ There is a pancake recipe that appears in *The Camper Van Cookbook* – it's a one-ring wonder and the kids love it. I'm not going to repeat it all here. Suffice it to say that you'll need flour (100g), 2 free range eggs, milk (about 300mls), a pinch of salt and some butter. Mix 'em all up with a whisk. Some will have you melt a little butter and add it to the mix but others won't. Some say let the batter rest, others don't. Anyway, get your frying pan hot, be prepared to make a mess of the first one and away you go. Lemon and sugar are what we first think of, but anything goes. Nutella might not be 'traditional' but it's flippin' lovely. Flippin'. See what I did there? Oh, never mind.

St David's Day, 1st March

Head to Wales for St David's Day and you'll find the locals showing off their cooking skills in fiercely competitive gastronomic bouts. They compete to make one of Wales' favourite national dishes, Cawl Cennin (a country soup made with lamb, pork, or whatever's best on the farm) at 'The Cawl Cooking Championships of the World… and Elsewhere' in Saundersfoot, Pembrokeshire and 'The Really Wild Cawl Competition', run by Julia Horton Powdrill in St David's. This is Julia's not-so-secret veggie option.

julia's VEGGIE CAWL

◀ FOR 4

4 POTATOES

2 ONIONS

2 LEEKS

1 SWEDE

4 CARROTS

2 PARSNIPS

2 BAY LEAVES

FEW SPRIGS OF THYME

30G BUTTER

1.2 LITRES VEGETABLE STOCK (OR WATER)

Cut up vegetables into good-sized chunks.

Melt the butter in a large saucepan and use to sweat down the onions and leeks on a fairly low heat for about 10 minutes (saucepan lid tightly on). Add the remainder of the veg and herbs and sweat for 5 minutes before adding the stock/water and bringing the mixture to the boil. Reduce to a simmer, put on a lid and cook for a further 30 minutes or so.

Season with salt and pepper and bring the mixture to the boil one more time before reducing to a simmer. Cook for 2 hours with the lid on, then take off the heat and allow the soup to cool a little. Remove the bay leaves and thyme stalks.

Serve with Welsh cheese and crusty bread, or even Welsh Rarebit.

St Patrick's Day, 17th March

It's amazing, isn't it, how everyone claims to be Irish on St Patrick's Day? I guess it's for the craic. But if you are genuinely Irish and have given up stout for Lent, then this is your one chance of a day off. It's a national holiday in Ireland and is celebrated all over the world with parades, merriment and much music and laughter. Some of the celebrations are huge, whilst others have been known to be quite small, like the one that used to be held in Dripsey, Cork. This was the shortest St Patrick's Day parade in the world ever and lasted just 100 yards as it 'wound' its way between the village's two pubs. My kind of parade.

CHUNKY colcannon

I won't claim Irish roots on any day of the year, despite having freckles and lots of reddish hair. But I am married to a bona-fide Irish woman and my kids hold Irish passports so there's reason enough to include a Paddy's Day recipe here. This is a great one to enjoy, whatever the date. Have it with some crispy bacon on top or with some meaty bangers on the side. Or try the colcannon alongside salmon filets. If you fancy a Colcannon cook-up, try the cakes on the next page.

FOR 4
5 LARGE MAINCROP POTATOES
HALF A SMALL SAVOY CABBAGE OR OTHER SPRING CABBAGE
LARGE KNOB OF BUTTER
6 TBSP MILK
4 SPRING ONIONS, CHOPPED

Peel the potatoes and cut them into chunks and shred the cabbage, discarding the core. Simmer the potatoes in salted water in a large pan until tender, 15-20 minutes, then drain.

Steam the cabbage for 3-4 minutes or until tender (if you have a steamer you can steam the cabbage above the spuds).

Drain the potatoes and return to the pan with the butter and milk and mash together. Stir in the spring onions and cabbage along with plenty of seasoning, particularly freshly milled black pepper. Re-heat and eat piping hot.

colcannon cakes
WITH SMOKY BACON

Start with the chunky colcannon recipe on page 69. Darina Allen, one of Ireland's best-loved food writers, suggests making colcannon with wild garlic, which also sounds delicious. Either way, serve with wholegrain mustard and a glass of very cold, slowly poured Guinness. If you are having this for breakfast, you can pop a poached egg on top or fry up some black pudding, no one will mind. Although, go easy on the Guinness.

◀ FOR 4

8 RASHERS SMOKED STREAKY BACON, CHOPPED
OLIVE OIL
SMALL BUNCH OF PARSLEY
ENOUGH CHUNKY COLCANNON FOR 4
DASH OF CREAM (ABOUT 2 TBSP)
PLAIN FLOUR, FOR DUSTING

Fry the bacon in a dash of olive oil in a frying pan until crispy and finely chop the parsley. Add the bacon to the pan of warm chunky colcannon (leaving the fat behind in the pan). Add the chopped parsley and cream and mix well.

Next grab a skimming spoon (a shallow spoon with holes in) or a slotted spoon and spoon the mixture into it. The idea here is to use the shape of the spoon as a mould to form a shallow spaceship shaped pattie that you don't have to handle (it'll be hot). Re-heat the pan of bacon fat and lightly dust the pattie with flour before popping it into the hot pan of sizzling bacon fat.

Once you've got a few patties in the pan, dust the top sides with flour and after 2-3 minutes of cooking, flip them over. Cook till crispy and piping hot. Add a little extra oil to the pan as you go, if needed – you should get about 8 cakes in total.

Coastal buildings

The feeble constructions of man are but a jot when you look at the black and imposing Cliffs of Moher in the west of Ireland or their proud and tall, white cousins in Dover. How about the coast itself? It's one long and complicated, ever-changing battle line that marks the end of our domain. With all the forces of nature battering it, we still think we can control it. How silly we are.

There are a bunch of coastal structures and buildings that are still worth taking another look at for their beauty, strength, the ideas behind them, or simply because of the sheer audacity of the project. And spring is a perfect time to go.

Top ten coastal structures:

1. THE EDEN PROJECT, **Cornwall** www.edenproject.com
Eden is spectacular and I love it. Go, go, go, whatever the cost!

2. TINSIDE LIDO, **Plymouth**
I love a lido. This is one of the best. It was opened in 1934 and has all the curvy excitement of the era. After much neglect, it was refurbished and re-opened in 1998. It's free and opens between May and September.

3. THE DE LA WAR PAVILION, **Bexhill-on-Sea** www.dlwp.com
If you like icons you'd be hard pressed to beat this coastal gem. It's been restored and now houses ever-changing art exhibitions and a good selection of salads. A Grade One listed grand day out.

The Eden Project, Cornwall

The Cobb, Lyme Regis

The De La War Pavilion, Bexhill-on-Sea

Blackpool Tower, Lancashire

4. SPINNAKER TOWER, Portsmouth www.spinnakertower.co.uk
Featuring Europe's largest glass floor. At 170 metres tall, it's an impressive
structure that has no real purpose except to provide you with great views.
A great big folly then.

5. WHITBY ABBEY, North Yorkshire www.whitbyabbey.co.uk
Wooooo! Scary. Whitby Abbey is a medieval joy, if that were possible.
With lovely views and an interesting history, it's inspired a few horrors.

6. BLACKPOOL TOWER, Lancashire www.theblackpooltower.co.uk
A Grade One listed building and top attraction. All kinds of seaside goings-on
and fine views. An icon in the north if ever there was one.

7. DURSEY ISLAND CABLE CAR, Beara Peninsula
www.bearatourism.com/bwdursey.html
I like an oddity and this is one of them. Once billed as Ireland's longest cable car,
it is, in fact, Ireland's only cable car. Get over to the island in a novel way and
mind the sheep – apparently they often travel by cable car too.

8. THE COBB, Lyme Regis
If you thought that the Cobb was one of those jetties that can take any kind of
pounding, think again. It's been rebuilt a few times. The latest was in 1824. This
remarkable coastal structure has been the scene of many movie moments, including
the one with the lady in the cape. Something to do with a French Lieutenant.

9. ST GOVANS CHAPEL, Pembrokeshire
Hermits will love this cutesy little chapel in a gash in a cliff – though
it can be a bit of a squeeze when there are a few of you.

10. HAWKER'S HUT, Morwenstow, Cornwall
The Reverend Hawker would amble down to his little driftwood hut
to enjoy uninterrupted views of the Atlantic, write poetry and smoke
opium. High times.

Spinnaker Tower,
Portsmouth

Get Some wind in your sails

Learn to sail a dinghy

I'm not a sailing sort. I don't go big on deck shoes and stripy t-shirts. Neither do I hang about in yacht clubs snorting and guffawing at every word the admiral deigns to throw my way. It's not my scene. Then again, I do like zipping over the water at speed and I do like the idea of travelling the world without damaging it in any way. Which is how come I found myself pootling off in the van to the south coast and making a weekend of learning to sail.

My friend Andy and I camped and cooked and got our RYA Dinghy Sailing Level One certificates at Shell Bay Sailing School in Studland. We had a brilliant couple of days and didn't capsize once (that's Level Two apparently). So hardly Olympic hopefuls just yet, but it was a fantastic way to learn a new skill and get more out of a visit to the coast.

The Royal Yachting Association (www.rya.org.uk) is the organisation responsible for training and administering sailing of all types in the UK. Their courses are available around the coast and they will teach you almost anything about sailing, yachting, windsurfing, jet skiing and powerboating, as well as navigation and seamanship. Qualify on a RYA beginner course (such as Dinghy Sailing Levels One and Two) and you can legitimately hire a small sailing boat at most rental centres around the coast and go off on your own. Or take a taster session, which means you can try your hand at sailing without the expense of a full course.

So why don't you give it a go? Who knows where it could end? Sailing across a silvery sea at the helm of a topper doesn't sound too bad…

Things to see in nature:
Visit a Seabird colony

The coastline of Britain and Ireland plays host to some of the largest and most spectacular seabird colonies in the world, providing breeding grounds for globally important populations of some species – around 90% of Manx Shearwater and 68% of all Gannet nest in our waters.

Visiting seabirds embark on huge journeys to our shores. The Arctic Tern travels a remarkable 44,000 miles from the Antarctic pack ice each way, each year – a journey that is unrivalled by any other bird species. Young Manx Shearwaters travel from British and Irish waters to the southern coasts of Brazil and Argentina in as little as a few weeks. Isn't that incredible? Some of these species are also surprisingly long lived – the oldest known Arctic Tern, nesting on the Farne Islands in Northumberland, has been making its 88,000 mile round-trip for 30 years, having flown well over 2.5 million miles in the process!

There are a wide range of seabirds to be seen on our coasts – the coastal cliffs of the north and west play host to Gannets, Razorbills, Guillemots, Puffins and Kittiwakes; the offshore islands to Gannets, Shearwaters and Petrels and sand and shingle banks on the east and south coasts to Tern and Gull colonies. Kittiwakes can also be seen nesting on piers and buildings in towns on the North Sea coast. A visit to any of these colonies is an unforgettable experience. And it's not all about the sight and sound of hundreds, sometimes thousands, of birds going about their business, but the smell too is something that will stay with you.

Visit www.rspb.org.uk for events, bird sanctuaries, wildlife reserves and identification guides. Or Google 'cliff bird colonies' to find the one closest to you.

Spring is the time of year when the rising sap and the first shoots of new growth make us yearn for food that's fresh and delicious. A little bit crunchy even. No more warming stews or hearty dollops of comfort. This is nosh for the get-up-and-go generation.

goat's cheese on toast
WITH THYME AND HONEY

This recipe is simple but perfect and it's always going to be different if you use local stuff whenever you make it.

FOR 2, OR 1 GREEDY PERSON
2 LARGE THICK-CUT SLICES OF SOURDOUGH OR OTHER RUSTIC BREAD
6 DISCS RIND-ON GOAT'S CHEESE (ABOUT 120G)
2 TSP THYME LEAVES
RUNNY HONEY, TO DRIZZLE

Preheat the grill.

Toast the bread under the grill on both sides until lightly golden. Top one side of each slice with three discs of goat's cheese. Scatter with thyme leaves and add some freshly ground black pepper to each one.

Grill the slices for 2-3 minutes or until the middles of the discs of cheese are molten. Drizzle each slice lightly with honey before devouring.

purple sprouting
WITH TWO EXTRAS

Does purple sprouting remind you of allotments and tweed trousers? It does me. My grandad used to grow it by the bucket load and I love it.

FOR 2
20 SPEARS (200G) PURPLE SPROUTING
OLIVE OIL
HALF A LEMON

FOR THE ANCHOVY MAYO
3 TBSP MAYONNAISE
2 ANCHOVY FILLETS IN OIL, DRAINED
  AND FINELY CHOPPED
1 TBSP SMALL CAPERS, DRAINED
2 TBSP CHOPPED PARSLEY
SQUEEZE OF LEMON JUICE

FOR THE ROASTED PEPPER SALSA
1 TBSP BLANCHED ALMONDS OR HAZELNUTS
1 ROASTED PEPPER FROM A JAR OR ROAST A
  SMALL RED PEPPER ON THE BARBECUE TILL
  BLACKENED
1 CLOVE GARLIC
2 GENEROUS PINCHES SWEET SMOKED
  PAPRIKA
2-3 TBSP OLIVE OIL

Bring a pan of salted water to the boil. Trim the tough ends from the broccoli. For the anchovy mayo, mix all the ingredients together with a generous grinding of freshly milled black pepper.

For the salsa, toast the nuts in a pan until golden, then cool and chop. Remove the skin from the pepper and finely chop the flesh. Peel and finely chop the garlic. Mix the nuts, pepper, garlic, smoked paprika and a pinch of salt. Add enough olive oil to make into a thick sauce.

Simmer the broccoli in the boiling water, drain and arrange on a platter or onto plates. Season and drizzle with olive oil and a squeeze of lemon juice. Eat with the mayonnaise and the salsa alongside.

cauliflower
CARBONARA

This isn't a real carbonara sauce but it has all the same flavours and is a great alternative to the usual cauliflower cheese. You could always cut the cauliflower into smaller florets and toss with cooked pasta. Try hard British cheeses too in the sauce – grated mature Cheddar or crumbled blue cheese both work well.

FOR 2

1 MEDIUM CAULIFLOWER
3 TBSP CUBED PANCETTA OR CHOPPED STREAKY BACON
1 SMALL CLOVE GARLIC, PEELED AND HALVED
4 GENEROUS TBSP CRÈME FRAÎCHE
BAY LEAF, PREFERABLE BUT NOT ESSENTIAL
5-6 TBSP GRATED PARMESAN (OR MIX HALF AND HALF GRATED PARMESAN AND
   GRATED PECORINO ROMANO)
WHOLE NUTMEG, TO GRATE

Bring a pan of salted water to the boil. Remove and discard the outer leaves and tough stalk from the cauliflower. Break the cauliflower curds into florets.

In a frying pan, dry-fry the pancetta or bacon till crisp, remove to a bowl. Drain off any fat from the frying pan and add the garlic halves and crème fraîche to it, slowly bring to simmering point and simmer gently for a few minutes.

Drop the cauliflower florets into the boiling water, bring back to simmering point and cook for 5 minutes or until just tender – add the bay leaf if you have one: it helps to minimise the stale cauliflower smell in the van.

Stir the cooked pancetta or bacon into the crème fraîche along with the grated cheese, a generous grating of nutmeg and some black pepper. Drain the cauliflower, tip back into its pan and toss with the cheesy sauce. Eat piping hot.

carrot and FETA PATTIES

Quick and delicious. Try these made with raw grated beetroot or parsnip too and vary the cheeses according to what's on board.

MAKES 10

4 SMALL-MEDIUM CARROTS
7 TBSP (100MLS) MILK
2 LARGE EGGS, YOLKS AND WHITES SEPARATED
100G SELF-RAISING FLOUR
1 TSP BAKING POWDER
4 TBSP CRUMBLED FETA
PINCH OF CRUSHED DRIED CHILLI FLAKES
OIL AND A SMALL KNOB OF BUTTER, FOR FRYING

Peel and coarsely grate the carrots. Whisk the milk and egg yolks in a medium bowl, to combine. Add the flour and baking powder, whisk in. Next stir in the grated carrots, the feta, chilli flakes and some seasoning.

In a clean bowl and using a clean whisk, whisk the egg whites to soft peaks and gently fold into the mixture.

Heat two tablespoons of oil and the butter in a frying pan till sizzling. Fry the fritters in the hot fat for 3 minutes on each side – you will need about two tablespoonfuls of mixture for each one. Serve hot from the pan.

asparagus, egg and baby leek
SALAD WITH CREAMY DRESSING

You may be lucky enough to find some wild asparagus but I'd make it a sure thing and get the freshest new season's shoots in April.

FOR 4, OR 6 AS A SIDE
3 LARGE EGGS
24 ASPARAGUS SPEARS
4 YOUNG TENDER BABY LEEKS
2 MEDIUM BEETROOT
SMALL HANDFUL TENDER TARRAGON SPRIGS

FOR THE DRESSING
2 TBSP OLIVE OIL
1 TBSP WHITE OR RED WINE VINEGAR
4 GENEROUS TBSP SOURED CREAM
2 HEAPED TSP DIJON MUSTARD

Bring a small pan of water to the boil, add the eggs, bring back to the boil and simmer for 7 minutes. Drain and leave to cool. Add a few centimetres of water to the pan, season with salt and bring to simmering point. Trim the ends of the asparagus spears and the baby leeks, halve the leeks lengthways. Simmer the asparagus and leeks, separately, for a few minutes each or till just tender, leave to cool.

For the dressing mix all the ingredients together and season.

Peel and thinly slice the beetroot – a flat-bladed peeler or very sharp knife are best for this.

Arrange the asparagus, leeks, beetroot and halved eggs on a platter. Drizzle with the dressing and scatter with the tarragon.

SPRING TO SUMMER risotto

Risotto is a wonderful versatile staple. Because it takes just one pan to cook the risotto you can use the other ring to make up your stock and keep it warm. In the autumn you can replace the carrot and green vegetables with 3 mugfuls (450g) of peeled, cubed butternut squash and use thyme as the herb. Top with fresh pesto or stir in some crumbled blue cheese at the end of cooking. Toasted pine nuts are a good extra too.

FOR 4

OLIVE OIL

GENEROUS SLICE OF BUTTER

2 SPRING ONIONS, TRIMMED AND SLICED

2 CARROTS, TRIMMED AND CHOPPED

1 CLOVE GARLIC, FINELY CHOPPED

350MLS (ABOUT 225G) RISOTTO RICE

SMALL TUMBLER OF WHITE WINE

1-1.2 LITRES HOT VEGETABLE OR CHICKEN STOCK

1 COURGETTE, TRIMMED AND CHOPPED

3 HANDFULS SHELLED PEAS OR SMALL, PODDED, BROAD BEANS

1 HANDFUL FINE GREEN BEANS, TRIMMED AND CUT INTO THREE

8 ASPARAGUS SPEARS, TRIMMED AND CUT INTO SHORT LENGTHS

2 TBSP EACH CHOPPED PARSLEY AND CHIVES

GRATED PARMESAN, TO SERVE

Heat 1 tablespoon oil and half the butter in a largish pan and cook the spring onions, carrots and garlic, covered, for 5-6 minutes until beginning to soften.

Stir in the rice. Turn the heat up high and pour in the white wine – bubble for a few minutes. Next add half the stock and bring everything to simmering point. Simmer the rice, uncovered and stirring frequently, for 10 minutes – adding more stock if needed. Stir in the courgettes, peas or broad beans, the green beans and the asparagus and bring back to a simmer. Cook, stirring and gradually adding the rest of the hot stock, for a further 7-8 minutes or until the rice is tender.

Stir in the remaining butter, herbs and some seasoning and take the pan off the heat. Cover the pan and leave the risotto to stand for 5 minutes before eating.

sea bass with olives
AND CAPERS

How about having an extra taste of the sea with this dish? Try some rock samphire. You should start seeing it from about April hanging on to rocky cliff faces. Hence the name, rock samphire. Simmer it for 7-8 minutes.

FOR 2

2 SHALLOTS (OR 1 SMALL ONION)
KNOB OF BUTTER
SMALL GLASS DRY WHITE WINE
2 SMALL SPRIGS ROSEMARY
3 TBSP OLIVE OIL, PLUS OIL FOR COOKING
SQUEEZE OF LEMON JUICE
2 TBSP CHOPPED PITTED OLIVES
1 TBSP DRAINED CAPERS, THE TINY ONES IF YOU CAN GET THEM
4 SEA BASS FILLETS
FLOUR, FOR DUSTING THE FISH

Peel and finely chop the shallots. In a pan, cook the shallots in half the butter, melted, till softened, this will take 7-8 minutes. Add the wine and the rosemary, bring to the boil and simmer to reduce by half. Discard the rosemary sprigs and whisk the 3 tablespoons of oil and the lemon juice into the onions. Next stir in the olives and capers and some seasoning, then set aside.

Heat the rest of the butter and a dash of oil in a frying pan. Season a couple of tablespoons of flour on a plate and dip both sides of the fish fillets in it briefly. Fry the fish over a highish heat for 3-4 minutes on each side until crispy and cooked through. Re-heat the sauce and spoon over the fish. Now it's ready to eat.

pan-fried sea trout with
LEMON PARSLEY SALSA

Well, the sea trout fishing season starts in springtime so what better way to celebrate this wild, great-tasting fish? Sea trout are basically brown trout that have gone to sea and are caught as they return to the rivers of their birth to spawn. Catching them is a tricky business as it's often done at night. So you'll get no tips from me other than go and see your fishmonger.

FOR 2
1 SMALLISH LEMON
20 BABY PLUM OR CHERRY TOMATOES
SMALL BUNCH FLAT LEAF PARSLEY
OLIVE OIL
2 SKINLESS SEA TROUT (OR SALMON) FILLETS, EACH ABOUT 150G
4 SLICES AIR-CURED HAM
BUTTER AND OIL, FOR FRYING

For the salsa, using a knife, peel the lemon removing and discarding as much of the pith as possible. Halve or quarter the tomatoes and chop the parsley, discarding the tough stalks. Toss the lemon pieces in a bowl with the tomatoes, parsley leaves, a dash of olive oil and a pinch of salt.

   Wrap each fish fillet in two slices of ham. Heat a knob of butter and a dash of oil in a frying pan and, when sizzling, fry each fillet for 4-5 minutes on each side until the ham is crisp and the fish is cooked through. Eat with the salsa.

scallops with
GARAM MASALA BUTTER

If you are heading to Rye Scallop Festival in early spring you'll know that the season there finishes at the end of April. So get them whilst you can, otherwise it's a long wait until late summer when they are back on. Go for hand dived if you can. It's a lot better for the bottom of the sea that way.

The scallops can also be griddled.

FOR 2

2 TBSP SOFT BUTTER
1 TSP GARAM MASALA
1 TBSP CHOPPED CORIANDER LEAVES
OIL, FOR COOKING
8 SCALLOPS
BREAD, FOR MOPPING UP JUICES (IDEALLY NAAN)

Mix the butter with the garam masala, coriander and a pinch of salt. Heat a frying pan till nice and hot and add a little oil.

Season the scallops and fry them for a minute on one side. Turn the scallops over and, as you do so, add the butter to the pan. Cook the scallops and butter together for a further minute, swirling the pan a couple of times so the scallops are thoroughly coated. Eat as soon as possible with bread.

cocktail for spring:
RHUBARB AND GINGER MARTINIS

A little something to warm you up this spring. When all is bursting into life but there's still a nip in the air this'll do it. Pink in colour and with a touch of ginger fire, you'll love it.

FOR 4

5 TRIMMED STEMS RHUBARB (400G)
3 TBSP CASTER SUGAR
1 TBSP FINELY CHOPPED ROOT GINGER
DRY VERMOUTH
VODKA OR GIN, WELL CHILLED

Cut the rhubarb stems in half lengthways, then into short lengths, about 2 cms. Tip the pieces into a pan, scatter over the sugar and ginger and add a tablespoon of water. Mix together then bring to simmering point and cook, partially covered, for 5 minutes or so until the rhubarb is tender. Leave to cool.

Strain the rhubarb in a sieve over a bowl. Keep the rhubarb to eat another time (delicious for breakfast with yoghurt) and tip the syrup into a jug.

Divide the syrup between four glasses and add a dash of vermouth to each. Top up with chilled vodka or gin, to serve.

SECRET WEAPONS: Recipes for all the family

Kids are funny creatures. They like something one day and then dislike it the next. As a parent it's frustrating. However, there is one sure-fire way of getting the kids to eat new things and that's by making food fun. If you pick mussels, they eat them because they have a stake in catching them. If you get them to make their own sushi rolls (like my friend Stefan does) then they will eat rice and raw fish. It's the same with fajitas and meatballs. That's why these recipes are our secret weapons…

family fajitas
WITH A SIMPLE SALSA

Everyone will find something to love when it comes to fajitas. Chicken, cheese, soured cream, griddled peppers. What's not to love? A mix and match feast with fans all around the table. Easy too …

◀ FOR 4 (2 ADULTS AND 2 CHILDREN)
OLIVE OIL
1 GREEN PEPPER
1 RED PEPPER
2 CHICKEN BREASTS
2 TSP SWEET, MILD SMOKED PAPRIKA
1 TSP GARLIC SALT
1 TSP FRESHLY GROUND BLACK PEPPER
8 SOFT FLOUR TORTILLAS
150MLS SOURED CREAM
100G MATURE CHEDDAR CHEESE, GRATED

FOR THE SALSA
2 TOMATOES
1 SMALL RED ONION
ABOUT 1 TBSP WINE VINEGAR
PINCH OF CRUSHED DRIED CHILLI
1 TBSP OLIVE OIL

First, make the salsa. Core and finely chop the tomatoes and peel and finely chop the onion, mix with the other ingredients in a small bowl. Season with black pepper.

Next, preheat a griddle over a medium-high heat. Core and slice the peppers lengthways and toss in a little oil. Griddle the sliced peppers until they have those lovely brown stripes on them but are still a little crunchy, 3-4 minutes. While that's doing, slice the chicken and make a rub by mixing the smoked paprika, garlic salt and black pepper, then toss the strips of chicken in the rub.

Once the peppers are done, griddle the strips of chicken for about 5 minutes or until cooked through. Meanwhile, warm the tortillas under the grill for about 30 seconds on each side

Finally, set out all ingredients on a big table and dive into the tortillas, the salsa, the peppers, the chicken, soured cream and grated cheese. But remember, it goes like this: soured cream goes onto the tortilla first, then chicken, then peppers, then a little salsa and finally some cheese. Roll up, folding the end in as you go and tuck in. Actually, forget that. Do it any way you please.

mart's meaty MEATBALLS

This is as close as we're ever going to get to a spag bol in this book. It's one of those dinners that everyone will love, even the kids, on a chilly spring evening. It's easy to make and will get better with time. So then you can make more than you need and save some for tomorrow.

◀ FOR 4

500G BEEF MINCE

2 ONIONS, FINELY CHOPPED

3 CLOVES GARLIC, FINELY CHOPPED

1 TSP HOT SMOKED PAPRIKA

1 LARGE EGG

4 TOMATOES

OLIVE OIL, FOR FRYING

1 TBSP TOMATO PURÉE

1 TBSP FINELY CHOPPED OREGANO, PLUS EXTRA TO FINISH

HALF A CUP (150MLS) HOT BEEF STOCK

300-400G DRIED TAGLIATELLE

HANDFUL GRATED MOZZARELLA

In a bowl, mix the mince, half the onion, two-thirds of the garlic, the paprika, egg and some seasoning, until combined. Shape into 24 round balls about 2-3 cm in diameter and place them on a plate or board. Set aside for 15-20 minutes.

Core and chop the tomatoes and get the rest of the ingredients lined up for the recipe.

Heat a dash of olive oil in a large deep-sided frying pan. Fry the meatballs in batches, over a medium heat, until browned all over. Remove them from the pan as they are ready.

Next, give the pan a wipe with kitchen paper and fry the other half of the chopped onion in a little oil until soft, 7-8 minutes. Add the rest of the garlic and fry for another minute or so. Stir in the chopped tomatoes, the tomato purée, oregano, beef stock and some seasoning.

Bring to the boil then simmer, uncovered, for about 10 minutes. At the same time bring a pan of salted water to the boil for the pasta.

After the 10 minutes, return the meatballs to the sauce and gently cook together for 10 minutes – cover the pan if the sauce is looking a little dry. Boil the pasta – check the pack for the cooking time. Preheat the grill on a high setting.

Sprinkle the mozzarella over the meatballs and put the pan under a hot grill for a couple of minutes until the cheese is bubbling. Drain the pasta. Dish up in big bowls, topping the pasta with the meatballs and sauce. Sprinkle with chopped oregano and tuck in!

Buono Appetito!

A TEA FOR SPRINGTIME: Darjeeling, the champagne of tea
To tea lovers, Darjeeling is the holy grail of fine teas, especially when it's the 'first flush' – the first leaves and buds to be picked once the new growth has begun after the spring rains. True Darjeeling cannot be grown or manufactured anywhere but in Darjeeling. Its subtle flavour and unique aroma are a result of the particular conditions of the area's soil and the climate in which the tea is grown. Cool temperatures and high humidity levels, together with the lofty terrain, produce the perfect terroir. The very best is picked above 4,000 feet.

MAKING THE PERFECT CUPPA
Use just off-the-boil water to preserve the Darjeeling's subtle flavours.

TEA APPRECIATION SOCIETY
I ♥ TEA
WWW.ilovetea.co.uk

rhubarb and CUSTARD POTS

It's a cheat but who wants to make custard on the hoof? Not me. I barely want to do any washing up. But that's beside the point. This recipe uses ready-made. Just make sure you recycle the can afterwards ('cos no one will know).

FOR 4
5 TRIMMED STEMS (400G) RHUBARB
4 TBSP CASTER OR SOFT BROWN SUGAR
2 TBSP GINGER CORDIAL
JUICE OF AN ORANGE
150MLS DOUBLE CREAM
250G THICK READY-MADE CUSTARD
4 GINGER NUT BISCUITS

Cut the rhubarb stems in half lengthways, then into short lengths, about 2 cms. Tip the pieces into a pan, scatter over the sugar and drizzle with the ginger cordial and orange juice. Mix together, then gently cook, partially covered, for 5 minutes or until the rhubarb is just tender. You want the pieces to retain their shape.

Leave to cool, then remove the rhubarb from the pan, leaving the cooking juices behind. Bubble the juices over a high heat until reduced, thick and syrupy.

When the rhubarb is cold, divide it between four glasses or pots. Whip the cream until it forms soft peaks, mix with the custard, add a quarter to each glass or pot. Just before tucking in, drizzle each one with rhubarb syrup and crumble a ginger nut biscuit on top.

SUMMER

Ice creams, clear skies and calm seas

Summer at last! If you're anything like me you'll have been waiting for the day when you can sack off work and head off to the coast. It's summertime. And the living, so they say, is easy. Mostly, I would argue, it is.

What I hanker for when the sun starts to reach its apex in late spring is a good old-fashioned summer holiday. I can't wait to get out there and get the sand between my toes, feel the sea salt curling my hair and watch the freckles appear on my forearms. These are all the signs of summer and a summer isn't a proper summer until I've seen and felt them.

Summertime brings so many simple pleasures. From giddy days at the end of the pier to sitting around a beach fire watching the sun go down, it's all about the senses. We feel the breeze. We see new places, wild flowers, happy faces. We hear the sound of the surf, the seagulls, the slap of the water on the sea wall. We taste the stuff we love more than anything: ice cream, chips with lashings of vinegar, the first season's strawberries, hand-picked samphire. All precious, all fleeting, all signs of summer.

So now is the time to make hay and enjoy every single, blessed moment. There are festivals to attend, music to dance to, drinks to be drunk and friends to laugh with. Finally, after the fresh mornings and chilly evenings of spring we can look forward to (and hope for) a few cloudless nights, a chance to sleep with the sliding door open and a sunset that will keep us warm for the remainder of the year.

Of course it's not always like that is it? There's every chance that my camper will be stuck for a few hours on the M6 on the way to somewhere or that it will give us a heart-stopping moment on the way to somewhere else. There will be rain and there will be anoraks. There may not even be a parking space when we get there. It's a fact of life. But I don't care. I can always go back another way, find somewhere better or chase that patch of blue sky until I'm sitting right underneath it. It's all part of a great big British summertime adventure. See you there.

Last one in the water is a sissy!

The ten best beaches

Every journey needs a destination. So what better than a very fine beach? The UK has so many. Whilst I will admit that I haven't been to every single one of them, in 25 years of surfing and exploring our coastline I've seen plenty enough of them to be able to spot a good one when I see it. This is my choice:

1. DERRYNANE BEACH, County Kerry

This beach has everything, which makes it my number one by a long, long way. It is the most westerly beach on the Ring of Kerry and is always worth a stop-off to see the white sands, low-tide pools and beautiful blue water. I've seen dolphins and sea otters here and caught mackerel from the rocks. There's a water sports centre, a great pub in Caherdaniel and a brilliant campsite nearby. Perfect.

2. LUNAN BAY, Angus

A gorgeous beach on the east coast of Scotland, just south of Aberdeen, with a sweep of clean white sands, lovely dunes and camping care of the excellent farm shop, Lunan Life. And you can ride a horse along the beach.

3. TORRISDALE, Sutherland

One of the most fabulous stretches of sand I have ever been to. It's remote with a river at each end and opportunities for wild camping. When I went I paddled across the River Naver to surf down the beach. My footprints were the only ones in the sand.

4. WOOLACOMBE, North Devon

A three-mile stretch of beautiful sand with many moods. At one end is Woolacombe, a laid-back holiday and surf town with surf emporiums, restaurants and bucket and spade shops. At the other is the quiet and very pretty Putsborough beach. In between is Middle Beach, a dune-backed stretch of sand that rarely gets busy.

5. BARRAFUNDLE, Pembrokeshire

This is one that gets rolled out all the time as the UK's most beautiful beach. Clean water, wooded cliffs, acres of great-to-explore dunes and gorgeous sands. It also has its own ruins. There's no parking at the beach so you'll have to walk in from Stackpole.

6. PORTH OER, Llyn Peninsula

They call this beach Whistling Sands because the sand squeaks beneath your feet when you walk on it. It's a crescent-shaped stretch of beach with lovely water and a little cafe. The nearby Porth Ceriad and Abersoch beaches give it a good run for its money though.

7. PORTHMEOR, St Ives

I love this beach because it was home for a while. White sand, blue sea and unbelievable light make it a Cornish cracker. Behind is the lovely arty town of St Ives with its Tate Gallery, twiddly-diddly shell shops and cobbled lanes. To the north side is the Island, a promontory with a small chapel on it. Great views, lovely walks, brilliant surf.

8. LULWORTH COVE, Dorset

The south coast's geological marvel Lulworth Cove has been wowing beach lovers forever with its horse-shoe shape and narrow entrance. To the west, Durdle Door, a magnificent rock arch, provides more great snorkeling and exploring and open-mouthed gawping.

9. SOUTHWOLD, Suffolk

There is everything to love about Southwold. A proper seaside town with proper beach huts (some have fetched as much as £40,000), a proper pier with proper amusements, a proper lighthouse and proper fish and chips.

10. EOROPIE, Isle of Lewis

A very long way from where I live, but it's a favourite, with crystal clear water, caves to explore at low tide, opportunities for dolphin spotting, beautiful dunes and even a lovely community play park for the kids. If you like peace and quiet this place is for you. Just fabulous, if you get the weather.

Derrynane

Torrisdale

Porthmeor

Durdle Door

Eoropie

The weather's here. Wish you were lovely.

SEND A POSTCARD HOME

Sometimes the world moves so quickly that some of the better things about going on holiday get lost along the way. One of them is sending postcards home. This is something that's as much a part of the great British seaside as donkeys, fish and chips and camping in muddy fields. Yet I'm afraid it might die out altogether before long. The problem is, with all these other ways of getting in touch, we just don't need postcards any more. They have become superfluous. How could a postcard compete against texts, emails and tweets? Well, I think they can.

Sending a postcard is a lovely thing to do, both for the sender and the recipient. As the writer you get to show the folks back home that you are thinking of them. You'll also get to stroll to the post office for stamps, spin through the racks at the bucket-and-spade shop, and spend half an hour scribbling neighbourly pleasantries, encoding sweet nothings, making up jokes or finding new words to describe the weather. Can you think of a nicer way to while away an afternoon?

Once you've popped your postcard in the post box, it'll just keep on giving – even in unexpected places. I can't say this for sure but I imagine postmen love a good postcard simply because they can read them. Who are we to deny them this pleasure? It must be awful being a postman with a sense of curiosity and nothing to read.

Finally, the postcard you send will land on someone's doormat, bringing with it a little slither of faraway sunshine and, hopefully, a smile. With any luck it'll spend a few weeks stuck somewhere where it'll be seen by anyone who happens by. They may even stop to read it, smirk at your smutty gag, speculate at the real meaning behind what's been written or feel inspired by the beautiful photograph. There. It's giving all over again! And that, I would argue, is a very nice thing.

So. Who have you been thinking about today? Nip out and send them a postcard. Before it's too late.

OOOH MRS! SAUCY SEASIDE SECRETS: Donald McGill was a graphic designer who was responsible for putting the saucy seaside postcard on the map. Between 1904 and 1962 he designed over 12,000 postcards. His designs sold over 200 million copies, yet he was prosecuted for obscenity in 1953 during a period of prudishness from local councils all around the British coast.

Beating the summer traffic

Here we go again. It's the summertime and it seems as if everyone else has got the same idea that you have. Make a dash for it! Head for the coast! Quick, let's all sit on the M5 for hours on end.

I am an old hand at traffic jams. I am also quite good at dodging them. Being an impatient soul, I would much rather be moving than not, even if I'm going off on some crazy track that's not even pointing in the right direction.

Sometimes you can't help but sit in a jam. Sometimes there is no way out. Happily though, this is another one of those occasions when you'll be jolly glad you're in a camper and not in a car. Stick the kettle on and settle down in the back. Heck, why not invite the neighbours round for a brew? (This will only work if you are well and truly stuck and NOT ACTUALLY MOVING.) But do not, under any circumstances, let anyone know that you have a Porta Potti in your van or everyone will want a go.

How to survive a traffic jam, the camper van way

PUT THE KETTLE ON. But only if you're not moving. Did you pack milk? Or enough cups for everyone? You won't forget it twice.
TURN THE IGNITION OFF. If you've stopped, turn it off. Yes, so there's a risk it won't start again but it's better than boiling your air-cooled engine isn't it? You'll save gas too.
PUT THE STEREO ON AND KICK BACK. There's nothing you can do, so go with it. No use getting all road-ragey and upset. It isn't going to help.
MAKE SURE YOU HAVE FOOD AND WATER ON BOARD. Well-fed campers are happy campers. We all know that. Pack supplies.
TELL BAD JOKES. A joke book that's cram-packed full of rubbish jokes can amuse children for unspeakably long times in traffic jams. Corny, but useful.
DON'T USE THE HARD SHOULDER. It's not worth the fine.

How to avoid traffic jams, the camper van way

GET UP EARLY, LEAVE LATE. The trouble with traffic jams is that they nearly always happen at busy times. The simple solution of course is to drive at the most unsociable times – during the night or very early in the morning. So you have to get up early? So what?

DON'T GO WITH THE FLOW. In many places, Saturday will be changeover day for holiday homes – and that means lots of traffic. Avoid it. You aren't governed by the time your cottage will be ready. Start your adventure on a Tuesday instead.

USE YOUR SMARTPHONE. Go online for live traffic updates: try www.trafficengland.com, www.trafficscotland.org and www.traffic-wales.com.

READ THE MAP AND FIND ALTERNATIVES. Maps are great. Get a good one, with lots of detail, and a world of possibilities opens up. Go cross country, stop at a village pub, take your time. You might make the journey last twice the time, but at least you'll be moving.

GO OFF-PISTE. Take a risk and get off the motorway as soon as it starts to clog up. There are other roads that will take you to your destination. Often motorways will have A-roads running alongside them. Take a quick detour and you might even learn something.

CONSIDER (FOR A MOMENT) GETTING A SAT NAV. The sexy-sounding lady has her uses – I'm told there's now a subscription that will enable you to avoid traffic hotspots as they happen. Sounds like sorcery to me.

DRIVE DEFENSIVELY. Keep a fair distance between you and the car in front and do your best to keep moving, even if all you're doing is creeping – that way, you won't get into that awful stop-start-stop that buggers up your clutch and your nerves. Other drivers may confuse your attempts at good sense as an opportunity. That's when it's OK to get cross.

Coastal camping spots

The very best on water

Stephen Neale, whose website 'Campsites on Water' details over 2,000 camping spots in the UK (www.cabbagemedia.com/campsites), has spent the last six years finding sites that are right on the coast. I'm not talking about a little way from the coast, or overlooking the coast. Stephen likes to be able to launch his canoe or cast his line pretty much from his pitch.

BEST FOR WALKING: Channel View, Somerset

www.breanfarm.co.uk/channel-view

Tourers can camp right up to the seawall, with direct access to the beach. The Brean Down alone is enough reason to visit – one of the most spectacular walks in Somerset.

BEST FOR A GALLOP: Beachcomber Camp Site, Northumberland

www.beachcomber-campsite.co.uk

Between Berwick and Holy Island, the beach seems to stretch for miles. If you forgot your horse, rent one (there's an on-site livery). No through traffic makes this is a safe site for kids, but bring plenty of beach games. Facilities are quite basic.

BEST FOR KIDS' CRABBING: Fleet Farm Camping and Caravan Site, Hampshire (tel: 02392 463 684)

A small campsite beside a tidal inlet (the beach proper is about five minutes away). Wet suits are handy if you fancy a dip in the creek. Excellent for crabbing and netting tiddlers. Boats and windsurfers can launch from the site too.

BEST FOR A SEA VIEW: Cliff House Holiday Park, Suffolk

www.cliffhouseholidays.co.uk

Cliff House overlooks the beach from several metres above sea level. It's also next to a nature reserve and on the edge of Dunwich Heath. This isn't the smallest of the sites, but it's a far cry from traditional holiday parks. Good facilities include a bar and restaurant, shop, playground and family games room.

BEST FOR DOLPHINS: Cae Du Campsite, Snowdonia
www.caeducampsite.co.uk
Dolphins visit at dusk and dawn. Enjoy sunset with the heat from your campfire. Driftwood litters the beach if you get low on fuel. The tranquillity is deafening.

BEST FOR DUNES: Hillend Caravan and Camping Park, Glamorgan
www.hillendcamping.com
On the Gower peninsula, this campsite rests beside 40km of coastline, beaches and wonderful sandscapes. Although it has become quite popular on the camping circuit, there's plenty of beach to go round.

BEST FOR WHITE SANDY BEACH: Traigh Na Beirigh, Isle Of Lewis
(tel: 01851 672 265)
If beach holidays are not your thing, then try Traigh Na Beirigh. All the trappings of a classic desert isle: white sands, turquoise sea, sunsets. Plus, amazing wildlife, a temperate summer climate, great hiking and wonderful Scottish hospitality. No electric or wifi either. Perfect.

BEST FOR SUNSETS: Invercaimbe Caravan and Campsite, Inverness-shire
www.invercaimbecaravansite.co.uk
A uniquely beautiful Scottish setting. The sheltered beach is good for fishing, paddling, swimming and boating. As this is a working croft, farm animals roam about freely. Nice for the kids.

BEST FAMILY RUN: Cranfield Caravan Park, County Down
www.cranfieldcaravanpark.co.uk
Tourers can park beachside with 40 pitches available. The park is right opposite Haulbowline Lighthouse, with great views of the beach and the Mourne Mountains.

How to put up a deck chair

Oh this is hilarious isn't it? But it's something that has flummoxed generations of bank holiday beach goers. Why? It's not that hard to put up a deck chair is it? The secret is to remember, from one year to the next, what it's supposed to look like when it's up. Remember that the shortest bar goes into one of the slots on the long bar, depending on how upright you intend to sit. That means that you must start with it facing towards the back of the deck chair, which is the side that has the slots in. The opposite end to the slots is the front of the deck chair and the other end of that is the back. See, it's simple. If you have the short bar on the front side of the deck chair, all will end in disaster. Got it? Oh never mind. Get someone else to help you.

How to put up a windbreak

Must we talk about this? It's like admitting defeat isn't it? Putting up a windbreak is an act that says many things. It says, 'It's too flipping windy to sit on the beach like in normal hot countries but we're going to do it anyway.' It also says, in our very small, overcrowded, island-dwelling way, 'I am creating my own little piece of England/Scotland/Wales/Ireland right here on this beach, whether you like it or not, so keep to your bit and I'll keep to mine.' And, as if that wasn't enough, it also says, 'I've got so little fun stuff to bring with me that I have room for this.'

Do you get that I don't like them? One of the reasons that I'm not a big fan of the windbreak is that they remind me of the days when I was a child and I had to carry one to the beach because my parents had their hands full with all the other crap they wanted to take to the beach. Windbreaks remind me of the pain of a middle England holiday. And the days before I learnt to pack light.

On the plus side though, a windbreak will allow you to sit on a beach and feel the benefit of the warmth of the sun when all around are drowning in a temperate sandstorm. It would also seem that they are extremely popular. What do I know?

So, to put them up? Bang 'em in with a mallet or a rock, whatever. I really don't care.

Make a drippy sandcastle

We've all filled a bucket with sand, turned it upside down and then whacked it with a plastic spade to remove the contents, haven't we? It's the number one technique for sandcastle building come summertime. And kids love it. But have you ever gone off-piste and made a drippy sandcastle? These are the Disney spectaculars of the sandcastle-building world and they don't come easy. It all depends on the quality of the sand and the amount of water in said sand.

First, half fill a bucket with water. Then top it up with the finest sand you can find at your beach – the finer the better. You should end up with a very watery, sandy sort of a mess, like very loose concrete. Grab a handful of this mess and hold it in your fist (be quick, or the water will fall out) then let the sand and water drip out of the bottom of your fist. As the sand lands and the water drains away you will be left with a small drippy-looking pile of sand that looks like the drips on a candle or like a very bad stalagmite.

As you repeat the process the pile of sand will grow and eventually may begin to resemble a tower from a Disney castle. For more elaborate buildings, make new towers. Continue in this way until you get fed up, or the tide comes in.

If you find you a have a talent for this, sandcastle competitions are held annually around the UK, including Woolacombe, Barry Island, Porthcurno, Westward Ho!, Folkestone and the Isle of Wight.

Swapping four wheels for four hooves

Where to ride a donkey on a beach

Hands up who can remember their first donkey ride? I can. It was at Weymouth. The donkeys there have been making kids smile for over a century. So I would have been following in a fine tradition when I had my early, freckle-faced and be-shorted adventures aboard Dobbin or Neddy way back in the seventies. As it happens, Maggie's Donkeys at Weymouth has won the Donkey Sanctuary's 'Top Working Donkey' prize. Pick from the charity's 2010 award winners (below) and you can rest assured that the donkeys your kids ride will have been well fed and well taken care of, with days off like the rest of us. Rightly so.

WEYMOUTH'S award-winning Beach Donkeys, Dorset. www.beach-donkeys.co.uk Operating on Weymouth beach from March to September, 11am to 5pm.

LLANDUDNO BEACH, Conwy County. www.greatorme.org.uk As typical a donkey-riding location as you could hope to get. Find them on the North Beach on sunny summer days, tides allowing.

BLACKPOOL BEACH, Lancashire. Where else? Two different owners operate from central pier and between them they can take tens of thousands of children out each summer. Friday is rest day.

PARKERS OF GREAT YARMOUTH, Norfolk. Donkey rides on Great Yarmouth sands run from Easter to the end of September.

SCARBOROUGH SOUTH BAY BEACH, Yorkshire. Award-winning donkeys provide rides all year round, weather permitting.

PAIGNTON (ON THE GREEN), Devon. The South West's finest group of donkeys provide rides from Easter to September.

DYMCHURCH DONKEYS, Kent. We understand that Floss is the most child-friendly donkey. Good for Floss.

THE DONKEY SANCTUARY (www.thedonkeysanctuary.org.uk) provides a loving home for retired, mistreated or abandoned donkeys at their site in Devon. You can visit at any time of the year. Just don't expect a ride. Pop a penny or two in the pot so they can live out their days in this pastoral paradise.

It's barbecue time

Oh yes. The summer is here. And it can only mean one thing…

I've written about barbecues before. I've written about how, somehow, men always take it upon themselves to 'take charge' at this point. I've also written about our moral duty as providers and protectors to perform the seriously complicated task of burning sausages. So I thought I'd covered barbecues.

That was until I went camping with my friends and neighbours from Horns Cross.

If you thought barbecuing was a social affair, take it from me that it isn't. It is a rite of passage. It is a very primitive form of feather preening and posturing, especially when oiled with beer. So, cooks beware. The company of others isn't always a good thing. The hyenas are coming. Better to light up the BBQ in the safety of the family unit, where the only wrath to encounter is that of the wife.

★ If you want a harmonious BBQ experience among men, nominate a chef and leave him alone.

★ Even so, men gathered together round a fire will be unable to resist offering 'constructive criticism'.

★ If you write cookbooks you will get scrutinised.

★ Standing around looking and offering tips is better fun than actually cooking.

★ If you show weakness they will take you down (but they will still eat your food).

Of course we all know that barbecuing doesn't have to be all frozen bangers and burgers and that there's really no excuse for flipping shop-bought lumps of gristle on a disposable that you discard the minute it's done. You, my cooking chums, will be able to do better than that. It ain't that hard to make your own burgers. And it certainly isn't a big chore to pack a bucket barbecue in your van, especially when you consider the awful waste of resources and energy that goes into making disposable barbecues. You won't be able to feed 40 of your best mates on a bucket barbecue either, which is every reason to celebrate.

Summertime! Whoopee. If it turns up, you'll be out there won't you? Take charge and put on a show to impress the campsite with your exotic smells and spices. Failing that, get some really fresh ingredients and do them some proper justice. I'll be impressed, even if the rest of the campsite isn't.

easy-peasy BURGERS

This is the real deal and anyone can make them. Swap the tiger rolls for soft white rolls or ciabatta if you're feeling posh, or rocket for lettuce if that's what's available. Heck, you don't even have to make the man jam, although nothing comes close to homemade chutney. If you must, get some relish from your nearest farm shop instead.

◀ FOR 4

1 RED ONION
1 CLOVE GARLIC
500G BEEF MINCE
1 TBSP FINELY CHOPPED THYME
1 TBSP FINELY CHOPPED PARSLEY
1 LARGE EGG
4 WHITE TIGER ROLLS
4 HANDFULS ROCKET
4 THICK SLICES EXTRA-MATURE CHEDDAR, TAW VALLEY TICKLER IF YOU CAN GET IT
TOMATO, CHILLI AND MUSTARD MAN JAM (OPPOSITE), TO SERVE

Peel and finely chop the onion and garlic and mix in a bowl with the beef, thyme, parsley and some seasoning. Crack the egg into the mixture and mix it through – don't be tempted to overwork the mix or the burgers will be tough, leave it a little rough. Now, with clean hands, form into four flat patties. Transfer the patties to a board or plate and leave them in the fridge, or somewhere cool, for half an hour.

Cook the burgers over a hot griddle or barbecue until done to your liking, 3-4 minutes on each side is a good guide. Serve in the tiger rolls with a handful of rocket, a thick slice of Cheddar and a big dollop of Man Jam.

tomato, chilli and MUSTARD MAN JAM

What on earth is Man Jam? Well, ladies, Man Jam is a cunning way to get your men folk to begin the long journey towards the art of making jams, jellies and marmalades. Like most things men understand, it's simple: call it something rugged and manly and they will make it. So whilst this is a chutney, calling it Man Jam makes it more acceptable, trust me. Let me tell you though, this Man Jam is proper butch. Oh yes. Chutney, you see, is something that makes life better. It's an extra dash of pizzazz that can make dull food sing, bring a boring sandwich to life and turn a dreary burger into a griddle pan masterpiece. And, as long as you've enough gas, you can make it in a camper van. So for us, it's perfect.

◀ FOR 8 BURGERS OR SANDWICHES (ALSO DELICIOUS WITH SAUSAGES)

6 RIPE TOMATOES
1 RED ONION
1 RED PEPPER
1 RED CHILLI
VEGETABLE OIL, FOR FRYING
½ TSP TURMERIC
1 TSP WHOLEGRAIN MUSTARD
2 SPRIGS ROSEMARY
100MLS WHITE WINE VINEGAR
8 TBSP CASTER SUGAR
1 TSP SALT

Peel, core and chop the tomatoes; peeling them is easy if you first soak them in boiling water for 1 minute, then drain them.

Peel and finely chop the onion. Core and chop the pepper and finely chop the chilli. In a pan, gently fry the red onion in a little vegetable oil for a few minutes.

Add the tomatoes, pepper, chilli, turmeric, mustard and sprigs of rosemary to the pan. Simmer everything gently, uncovered, for about 30 minutes or until the tomatoes are reduced to a pulp.

Next, stir in the vinegar, sugar and salt and continue to simmer until all the liquid has evaporated: this will take 15-20 minutes. Remove the rosemary sprigs, then tip the Man Jam into a jar (or bowl), cool and cover.

barbecued chicken with
LEBANESE STYLE SALAD

FOR 6

12 SKIN ON, BONE-IN CHICKEN THIGHS

JUICE OF 4 LEMONS

3 TBSP OLIVE OIL

2 TSP GROUND CUMIN

4 CLOVES GARLIC, CRUSHED

GREEK YOGHURT, TO SERVE

FOR THE SALAD

2 PITTA BREAD

HALF A CUCUMBER

3 SPRING ONIONS

20 CHERRY TOMATOES

3 LITTLE GEM LETTUCES

HANDFUL FLAT LEAF PARSLEY LEAVES

HANDFUL MINT LEAVES

GENEROUS HANDFUL WALNUT PIECES

JUICE OF A LARGE LEMON

3 TBSP OLIVE OIL

2 TSP SUMAC, PLUS EXTRA TO SPRINKLE

Put the chicken into a large bowl. Whisk together the juice of the four lemons, the olive oil, ground cumin, crushed garlic and some seasoning. Pour over the chicken and turn the chicken a few times. Leave to marinate in a cool place for 30 minutes (or longer is fine, if everything is chilled). Fire up the barbecue.

Toast the pitta breads under the grill (or on the barbie) for 1-2 minutes on each side or till nicely golden. Leave to cool. Halve the cucumber lengthways, slice and put into a large bowl. Trim and slice the onions, halve the cherry tomatoes, chop the lettuces, add to the bowl and mix. Roughly chop the parsley, mint and nuts.

In a small bowl, mix the juice of the large lemon, the olive oil, sumac and some seasoning. Break the pitta into bite-sized pieces.

Barbecue the chicken for 20-25 minutes, turning, until cooked through. Toss the salad with the lemon dressing, then layer on a platter with the chopped herbs, nuts and toasted pitta pieces. Finish with a generous sprinkle of sumac, eat with the chicken and some Greek yoghurt on the side.

BARBECUED pork chops with fennel, ginger and PEACH COUSCOUS

FOR 6

275MLS (ABOUT 200G) COUSCOUS

OLIVE OIL

1 RED ONION, CHOPPED

1 SMALL BULB FENNEL, TRIMMED AND CHOPPED

2 TSP FENNEL SEEDS

2-3 TSP GRATED ROOT GINGER

2 RIPE BUT FIRM PEACHES (OR NECTARINES)

SMALL HANDFUL BASIL LEAVES

6 FAT JUICY BONE-IN PORK CHOPS

Fire up the barbecue (or a griddle). Tip the couscous into a large bowl, add 350mls boiling water and set aside.

Heat a tablespoon of oil in a frying pan and fry the onion, fennel and fennel seeds for 8-10 minutes or until softened. Stir in the ginger and cook together for a further minute or so, then take off the heat. De-stone and chop the fruit then shred the basil.

Rub the chops in olive oil and seasoning and barbecue over the hottest part of the fire for a few minutes on each side, then move the chops to the edges of the fire to cook for a further 8-10 minutes or until cooked through, turning them now and then.

Fluff up the couscous and stir in the onion and fennel mixture, the fruit, basil, a slug of olive oil and some seasoning. Toss together and enjoy with the chops.

CURRIED PORK kebabs

This is a throwback to holidays of old in the Canaries. As you may have noticed, it's all about the spices for those Canarians. They don't hold back either. This recipe is perfect for the barbecue but you can cook them under the grill or over an open fire if you feel so inclined. Bamboo skewers (to make the kebabs) will need soaking in water for about 30 minutes. My tip is to fill up an empty screw-top wine bottle with water, put the skewers in and screw the lid on to keep from floating. Serve the kebabs with a tomato, garlic and red onion salad.

◄ MAKES 8 LARGE KEBABS
1KG BONELESS PORK CHOPS
1 CLOVE GARLIC, FINELY CHOPPED
100MLS OLIVE OIL
JUICE OF 1 LEMON
1 TSP PAPRIKA
1 TSP CURRY POWDER
1 TSP GROUND CUMIN
LEAVES FROM A SMALL BUNCH THYME, FINELY CHOPPED
SMALL BUNCH CORIANDER, FINELY CHOPPED

Cut the meat into strips of about 2 cm. Mix all the other ingredients to make a marinade, then marinate the meat strips for at least an hour and a half, making sure that the meat is completely coated.

Skewer the strips of pork and barbecue (or grill) them for about 5 minutes each side until browned and cooked through.

squid in minutes, with
PEPPER, ORANGE AND CHILLI

To be eaten tender, squid needs to be cooked very quickly or very slowly, nowhere
in-between will do. It is also good cooked on a griddle. Either way, you are aiming
for squid that is slightly charred at the edges.

FOR 2

8 SMALL OR 4 MEDIUM-SIZED SQUID, PREPARED,
    HOODS AND TENTACLES SEPARATED (SEE BELOW)
2 TBSP OLIVE OIL, PLUS LITTLE EXTRA
1 RED PEPPER, DESEEDED AND CHOPPED
½ TSP CRUSHED DRIED CHILLIES OR 1 RED CHILLI, DESEEDED AND FINELY CHOPPED
ZEST AND JUICE OF A SMALL ORANGE
SWEET SMOKED PAPRIKA, TO SPRINKLE

Fire up the barbecue.

To prepare your squid, first cut the head off. Next cut the tentacles off the squid head
and set them aside. Discard the rest of the head. Cut the body pouch open on one side,
then give it a good rinse out, discarding the insides. Slice into thick strips and then,
using a small sharp knife, score the underside of the squid in a criss-cross pattern. Toss
the squid in a bowl with a drizzle of olive oil and some seasoning.

Add a splash of oil to a barbecue-proof frying pan and fry the red pepper until
softened and charred at the edges, 5 minutes or so.

Tip the cooked pepper into a largish bowl and mix with the two tablespoons of oil,
the chilli and the orange zest and juice.

Put the pan back on the barbecue, heat till smoking hot. Fry the pieces of squid in
two batches, scored side down, for about a minute per batch. Throw the squid tentacles
into the pan and stir-fry for 30 seconds. As the squid is ready, add it to the bowl with
the pepper. Toss everything together with a twist of sea salt and pile into bowls. Sprinkle
with smoked paprika and eat as soon as possible.

barbecued fish parcels
WITH LEMON BASIL BUTTER

This is super simple and very quick. Use whatever fish is available.

FOR 4
SOFT BUTTER
4 WHITE CHUNKY FISH FILLETS, EACH ABOUT 150G
1 LEMON, FINELY SLICED
HANDFUL BASIL LEAVES

Lightly butter the non-shiny side of four large squares of foil. Place a fish fillet on one side of each square, season then top with a couple of slices of lemon, a few basil leaves and a small knob of butter.

    Make a parcel of each square by folding the empty half of the foil over the fish and pinching the edges together. Barbecue for 10-12 minutes, then give everyone their own parcel of fish and delicious juices to open and enjoy.

barbecued lobster
WITH THAI FLAVOURS

Killing lobster humanely can be an issue if you're out and about. The best way, if you were at home, would be to put them in the freezer for a couple of hours. However, freezers are hard to come by, so you may have to beg or buy some ice, then pack the lobster in a cool box for two hours.

FOR 2
2 LIVE LOBSTERS, CLAWS TIED
2 TBSP THAI GREEN CURRY PASTE
400ML TIN COCONUT MILK

FOR THE SALAD
2 SMALL TO MEDIUM CARROTS
1 SMALL NEARLY RIPE MANGO
JUICE OF A LIME
1 TBSP THAI SWEET CHILLI SAUCE
1 TBSP RICE VINEGAR
1 TBSP SOY SAUCE
HANDFUL CORIANDER LEAVES

After two hours in ice (see above), insert a large sharp knife into the middle of your lobster's head – there is a natural cross on the top where the vertical and horizontal creases meet. This is done in seconds and destroys one of the main nerve centres. Immediately, turn the lobster over and cut all the way through the midline on the underside to cut in half. Discard the green parts. Same goes for the second lobster.

In a large bowl or clean bucket, whisk the curry paste with the coconut milk. Add the lobster halves and turn them in the marinade, leave aside in a cool place for 30 minutes (or longer is fine if everything is chilled). Fire up the barbecue.

Peel the carrots, halve them and then slice into thin matchsticks – put them in a bowl. Peel and de-stone the mango and slice the flesh into thin strips, add to the bowl with the rest of the salad ingredients. Toss together.

Barbecue the lobster halves for 3-4 minutes on each side, basting with the marinade. Eat hot, with the salad. Use the back of the spoon to crack open the claws. You'd think it wouldn't work, but it does.

AUBERGINE, pepper and HALLOUMI KEBABS with LEMONY houmous

This recipe is a simple veggie alternative for the BBQ that will serve two. Alternatively, they will work equally well as an accompaniment to lamb, to serve four.

MAKES 4 KEBABS
2 MEDIUM AUBERGINES
OIL, FOR FRYING
ABOUT 3 TBSP HOUMOUS
ZEST OF A SMALL LEMON
1 TBSP SMALL CAPERS, DRAINED
3 ROASTED RED PEPPERS, FROM A JAR, SLICED INTO 12 STRIPS
125G HALLOUMI, CUT INTO 12 THIN SLICES
12 BASIL LEAVES

Preheat the barbecue. If using bamboo skewers, soak four in cold water for 30 minutes to prevent them from burning. Otherwise, use metal ones.

Trim off and discard the tops from the aubergines, then slice the aubergines lengthways – you want the slices to be about ½ cm thick and you should get six slices from each. The skinnier slices from the edges are no use for this recipe but keep them to chop and fry to add to a salad.

Fry or griddle the 12 slices, in batches, in oil, for a few minutes on each side, or until tender, then leave them to cool briefly. Mix the houmous with the lemon zest and capers.

Lay a cooked aubergine slice, lengthways, on a board in front of you. Place a strip of pepper, a piece of halloumi and a basil leaf onto the top end of the slice and then, starting at the top, roll the slice towards you. Put to one side and repeat twice more. Thread the three rolls onto a skewer. Repeat with the rest of the ingredients and the other three skewers. Barbecue for 6-8 minutes, turning halfway and eat with the lemony houmous.

three ways with CHICKEN

I don't know about you, but my relationship with the humble chicken breast passes through many phases. It's one of those foods that always seems to end up in the cooler with no real purpose or plan. It's a fall back. But, even worse than that, it's a fall back with a shelf life. Happily, though, once you fire up the barbie, there are a few things you can do with your chicken breasts that will stop them from being mild-mannered moochers and turn them into the superbirds they should be.

Give it a rub-a-dub
Rubs are great for chicken. You can make your own with a touch of freshly ground black pepper, sea salt and a few dried herbs. Try tarragon or oregano. Otherwise, smoked paprika will add a wonderfully dark and spicy Spanish flavour, whereas ras-el-hanout will give it a subtle Moroccan brightness that goes really well with couscous and citrus flavours. Whatever you go for, strips of rubbed chicken will cook quickly and can be griddled, grilled or barbecued.

Stuff it
Let's take a trip down memory lane here and go back to the times when our campers were born. How about a take on chicken kiev? It's not so hard to mix up a little garlic and some butter and parsley and stuff yer chicken breast. First, using a sharp knife, make a pocket along one side of each chicken breast, then stuff your butter and garlic and herb mix inside. Then wrap in bacon and grill. Alternatively, wrap in kitchen foil, season and put on the barbecue. Yum! Moist garlicky chicken! Also try stuffing with green or red pesto (try the home-made recipe on page 58) or even just a few fresh herby mixes – chopped tomato and basil, lemon and tarragon.

Marinate it
Another way of getting your chicken breast super-duper lovely is to marinate it. Simple stuff like honey, mustard and Tommy K can make a dull chook sing, whereas a little oil, some cumin, chilli and seasoning will keep it moist and tasty. How about soy sauce, chilli flakes, a dash of lime and some brown sugar? Leave it for an hour or so then griddle or grill it.

ROCKY ROAD bananas

Kids love these – gooey banana, sticky marshmallow and chocolate melted into one yummy pud. Something to cook at the end of a barbecue feast in the dying embers of the fire.

FOR 4
8 MARSHMALLOWS
8 SQUARES MILK CHOCOLATE
4 BANANAS
4 TSP GOLDEN SYRUP
2 DIGESTIVE BISCUITS

Chop the marshmallows and chocolate. Using a sharp knife, slice along the length of each banana on the curved inside – through the skin and flesh but not through the skin on the other side.

Place one of the bananas cut side upwards on a square of foil and prise apart the cut you have made to create an opening for the stuffing. Stuff the banana with marshmallows and chocolate. Drizzle with golden syrup and wrap the foil around the banana to enclose it completely. Repeat with the other three.

Barbecue the banana parcels for 15-20 minutes over a low heat. Chop the biscuits into bite-sized pieces. When ready, open up the parcels, sprinkle with the biscuits and enjoy.

Ian says, 'Cool it!'

The amazing beer can cooler

Sometimes the best things come out of the blue. It was that way when my mate Ian from SW Classic VWs revealed his method of cooling cans of beer* on long journeys. We were trying to work out whether or not we could cook on the heat exchangers (I managed one lukewarm sausage after 10 miles at 40 mph, so, the answer is, maybe, but not really) and were peering underneath a 2.0 litre late bay when he suddenly snapped his fingers and said, 'Did you know that you can fit beer cans in the nozzles from the cool air vents in the dash?'

'What?' I asked. 'Are you serious?'

'Yeah. They fit perfectly. And when you drive, cold air cools the cans from the bottom.'

'Clever.'

'Oh yes. Stuff them in. When you get there, crack a cold one.'

He's not joking either. Beer cans do fit in the nozzles. They will cool as you drive along. And they can't fall out, or disappear into the dashboard, because there is a bend in the nozzle that keeps them in place until you need them.

And that, my friends, is German engineering at its best (whether intentional or otherwise).

*This method also works for other types of drinks cans, soft drinks included.

In search of the finest ice cream

How do you go about trying to find the UK's best ice cream? Who's to say that a Hockings Oyster, eaten on a sunny day on Westward Ho! beach, is any better than a Dulaval on a wet weekend in Whitby, after an argument with your partner, or a Splitscreen ice cream at a VW festival? There's no telling.

But an ice cream is about the experience, more than the taste ... In 2010 I was away from home for five weeks in my van. At the end of the trip my family came to 'pick me up' in St David's, Pembrokeshire. There, at a restaurant called The Bench, we sat in the sun and wolfed down four of Gianni's fine artisan ices. I can't even remember which of the many flavours I had. I just know that it was delicious. Really delicious. So that's my finest ice cream.

What's yours?

Tombstoning

Once upon a time we used to chuck ourselves off cliffs and into the blue without a care in the world. We had a secret diving cove that we'd paddle our surfboards to and then dare ourselves to jump off the highest ledges. It was the very best fun. But somewhere along the way, the simple sport of jumping off things into the sea has got itself a bad name. Between 2004 and 2008, 12 people died jumping into water in the UK, with dozens of others suffering from serious, life-changing injuries. Summer fun has become 'tombstoning' and has been vilified by the press. Yes, there are risks with jumping off things, especially if you don't know what's down there. But only a fool would leap into dark water with no guarantee of the landing.

Before you jump

Check for hazards in the water (submerged rocks and obstacles need to be scoped, ideally with a mask and snorkel). Check the depth of water, currents that could sweep you into deeper water or away from your exit point, and shifting tides (remember, tides go in and out very quickly, meaning the water depth changes too). Jump feet first with your hands folded against your chest – don't hold your nose. Don't jump if you've been drinking.

Looking for somewhere to do it?

Some councils ban jumping from their piers and jetties (for safety reasons) so take heed. One option is to do it from places that are safe, like diving boards at seawater lidos. With lifeguard cover you'll still have fun, with minimum risk. Alternatively, try it with a professional coasteering company first. They do it safely every day. Once you know what you're doing, check out *Wild Swim* by Kate Rew and *Wild Swimming: Coast* by Daniel Start for inspirational jumps around the coastline.

One, two, three, jump!

I want to be free

Living and cooking in a camper van is all about freedom, right? So why not go the whole hog by getting naked? It is and can be a marvellously liberating experience. There is a strong argument to say that you can only be truly liberated when you've cast aside your bodily hang-ups and stepped into the non-textile world. I tend to agree, although I'm shyer than most.

SEASIDE SECRETS: If you want to get naked without the hassle (and the funny looks), there are a number of beaches where naturism is accepted. So whilst there is no law against nudity on any beach, go elsewhere and you're on your own:

- BUDLEIGH SALTERTON (West End) in Devon
- STUDLAND BAY, near Swanage, Dorset
- BRIGHTON EAST BEACH and FAIRLIGHT GLEN, Hastings, East Sussex
- ST OSYTH in Clacton-on-Sea, Essex
- HOLKHAM BEACH in Wells-next-the-Sea, Norfolk
- LEYSDOWN-ON-SEA at the eastern end of the Isle of Sheppey, North Kent
- CLEAT'S SHORE on the Isle of Arran, South West Scotland
- GUNTON SANDS (Corton Beach) in Lowestoft, Suffolk
- MORFA DYFFRYN in Gwynedd, on the Welsh coast

SKINNY-DIPPING

Discretion is, and should be, the better part of valour. Let's face it, if you get naked you will attract attention. But skinny-dipping is really liberating and I'd rather go naked than wear a pair of budgie smugglers any day. Skinny-dipping can be done anywhere at any time but I would dare to suggest that quiet coves, deserted sands and warm water are prerequisites for a naked dip. As with all 'wild swimming', make sure you are fit enough, that you understand the local conditions and that you can handle the cold water. Now get your kit off. The water's lovely.

sea bass with a simple fresh
TOMATO AND BASIL SAUCE

I know what it feels like to stare at a bit of fish and wonder what to do with it. You don't want to deep fry it and you can't be bothered to turn it into a curry. It's a fishy quandary. But if you've got yourself a gorgeous piece of fresh sea bass you wouldn't want to mess with it too much anyway. So, here's one simple solution. Serve with a green salad drizzled with balsamic vinegar.

◀ FOR 2

BUTTER AND OLIVE OIL, FOR FRYING
1 RED ONION, FINELY CHOPPED
8 RIPE TOMATOES, ROUGHLY CHOPPED
PINCH OF SUGAR
2 SEA BASS FILLETS
HANDFUL BASIL LEAVES, CHOPPED

Heat up a frying pan and add the butter and a glug of olive oil. Gently fry the red onion for 4-5 minutes. Stir in the chopped tomatoes and the pinch of sugar and cook together for a further 2 minutes. Tip the tomato sauce into a bowl, season and set aside.

Wipe the pan out with kitchen paper and return it to the heat with a little more butter and oil. Season the fillets and place them in the pan, skin side down first, to cook for 3 minutes. Turn and cook the fillets for a further minute, or a bit longer if they are big. Once the fish is cooked return the tomato sauce to the pan, sprinkle with the basil and heat together for a further minute or so.

Serve up straight away and enjoy!

Best fish and chips?

Summer wouldn't be summer without fish and chips overlooking the sea. It's the original fast food. It's cheap, convenient and easy to eat. So where do they serve the best fish and chips in the UK? The answer, I will tell you, is that I don't know. I copped out of actually going to visit all the seaside fish and chip restaurants in the UK, because I like the shape I'm in and don't have the next two years to spare. But I did act on a whim and drove my van 800 miles to what I thought was going to be the 'most remote fish and chip shop in the UK' at Port Nis on the Isle of Lewis. That's about as far as you can get in the UK without falling off. Once we got there it took us no time to realise the shop wasn't there. Or was hiding. So much for research.

Anyway, despite this disappointment we found a restaurant called Port Beach House, where they served fresh fish and chips, with mushy peas and tartare sauce (and a smile), as well as line-caught sea bass, creel-caught langoustines, Isle of Lewis lobster and all sorts of other fresh and local fishy fancies. And I loved it because they actually did very good fish and chips and – most importantly – did everything a good chipper should*:

* If you are by the sea it must be local
* It must be sustainable
* It must be freshly cooked, not frozen
* It must be delicious
* It must not be served in a polystyrene carton or with a plastic chip fork
* It must be served by nice people

*my list

FISH AND CHIPS:
a recipe for a seaside supper, the camper van way

If the chippy is closed, don't panic. You can have crispy-coated fish and chips in your van without breadcrumbs or a deep fat fryer. All you need is cornflakes. It's one of those age-old answers to an age-old problem.

FOR 2

2 HANDFULS CORNFLAKES

1 TBSP FINELY CHOPPED PARSLEY

1 TBSP FENNEL SEEDS

1 MEDIUM EGG

2 GOOD SIZED LINE-CAUGHT POLLOCK FILLETS

MAYONNAISE AND CAPERS, TO SERVE

FOR THE CHIPS

BUTTER AND VEGETABLE OIL, FOR FRYING

2 CLOVES GARLIC, PEELED

6 MEDIUM POTATOES, DICED INTO 2 CM CUBES (PEELED OR UNPEELED IS FINE)

1 RED ONION, FINELY CHOPPED

8 CHERRY TOMATOES

For the chips, first, heat a knob of butter and a couple of tablespoons of oil in a frying pan. Add the garlic (it's whole so you can fish it out later) and the cubed potatoes and season well. Fry gently for about 10 minutes, turning regularly. Now stir in the onion and cook together for 5 minutes. Next, add the cherry tomatoes and keep turning everything over the heat for a further 5 minutes or until the spuds are golden.

Meanwhile, crush the cornflakes in your hand into a bowl until they are finely crumbed. Add the parsley, fennel seeds and a pinch of salt and pepper. Towards the end of the cooking time for the chips, get a second pan warm to cook the fish in.

Melt a knob of butter in the pan with a glug of oil.
Next, crack the egg into another bowl and beat it with a fork for a few moments. Dip the fillets in the egg and then coat with the cornflake mixture. Place in the pan skin side down and cook on a medium heat for about 3-5 minutes before turning over and continuing to cook for the same time on the other side.

Serve the crispy fish with the chips, a dollop of mayo and maybe a few capers too.

The coastal explorer

Sometimes it's nice to sit and look at the sea. At other times you simply must get out of the van and get involved with it. There are nooks and crannies to explore, methods of getting across the water to try out and all manner of ways of making your time at the coast that much better. Here are a few ideas...

SEE IT ON A SIT-ON

As a very small Sea Scout, sometime in the early eighties, I found it to be a real struggle to get any excitement out of canoeing on a murky, gnat-infested Thames. But now I've had the chance to take to the water on a sea kayak and do some coastal exploring, I see it differently. The kayak is a way to see the treasures in a way a boat could never match.

The sit-on-top sea kayak is basically an open-topped, plastic-moulded canoe that one or two people can paddle. They are unsinkable because they cannot fill up with water and can handle a bit of white water. They are also very easy to paddle. An added bonus is that they are stable enough to get back on to if you fall out. There are lots of places to hire sit-ons around the coast, but I would recommend going out with a guide who can show you how to do it and where to do it – at least at first. As usual the locals will know where you can go safely, how far you can paddle, what the tides are doing and what kind of weather to expect.

I went with my mates at TYF in Pembrokeshire as part of a coastal explorer day (www.tyf.com). We paddled into caves, into secluded coves, across sheltered bays, through arches and saw, for the very first time, what's at the foot of the cliffs (in Pembrokeshire it isn't shopping trolleys I can assure you).

STAND UP AND BE COUNTED

Stand-up paddle surfing, or SUP, as it's more commonly known, is the enfant terrible of the surfing world. Compared to standard surfing, the paddle gives you more acceleration, which means you can catch waves earlier. You also get a better view of the water, can see sets appearing earlier and can easily cover more ground than a traditional surfboard. It's an advantage we'd all like.

As is often the way with board-based sports (like kiteboarding, windsurfing and skateboarding), SUP has partly grown out of a need to find a surfing-like experience on days when there is no surf. Any lake, pond, harbour or body of water is suitable, which explains why the sport has developed so quickly. It's not a million miles away from outrigger canoeing and, at a push, even the good old British pastime of punting.

The basics

SUPs are generally bigger than standard surfboards because they need to be a stable platform from which to ride. That means they range, typically, from about 9ft to 12ft and are often as wide as 34 inches. However, they aren't cheap. A standard set-up will cost about £1,000.

To paddle, you stand with your feet parallel and use a long single paddle.

Learn to SUP

The British SUP Association has devised a basic certificate in SUP, The BSUPA Level 1, which is designed to get complete beginners in the water safely and effectively. It is a one-hour course and can be taken at a few locations around the UK. Visit www.bsupa.org.uk for more information.

SNORKELLING

Summer is by far the best time to go snorkelling in the UK. This is because the water will be warmer than at other times of the year and the visibility will be better. When there is surf or onshore winds or lots of rain the visibility in the water can be severely hampered by silt and sand. A few days of calm weather and gentle breezes will allow the water to clear and be at its best. Sand from beaches will often cloud the water, so reefs, points and promontories will be among the best places to go.

The water is relatively cold in the UK. That means that you'll need a wetsuit if you intend to snorkel for any length of time without catching hypothermia. Whilst a quick dip will be OK in swimmers, spending more than a few minutes with your head in the water will feel very different. On top of that you'll need a pair of flippers, a mask and a snorkel. That's it.

Renowned snorkelling sites in the UK are at:

* **CONGER ALLEY**, Argyll
* **BAGGY POINT**, North Devon
* **LUNDY ISLAND**, off the coast of North Devon
* **PRUSSIA COVE**, Cornwall
* **KIMMERIDGE BAY**, Dorset
* **DURDLE DOOR**, Dorset
* **THE FARNE ISLANDS**, Northumberland
* **CILAN HEAD**, North Wales
* **NORTH LANDING**, Yorkshire

A DIVER'S PARADISE

I absolutely love diving. The thing is, once you go, you'll want to see more. And with cold-water reefs, cave systems, wall dives, drifts, gullies and shallow bays, there's a lot to see around our coast. The area around Plymouth provides some of the UK's best shoreline diving, with vivid colours coming from a thick carpet of vegetation and a wide range of sea creatures. Large numbers of thornback rays, congers, lobsters and crabs throng the seabed. Alternatively, visit the Farne Islands and you can also expect some inquisitive nibbling at your fins – the islands have a population of up to 6,000 grey seals.

SEASIDE SECRETS: There are more wrecks per mile of UK coastline than anywhere in the world, from the famous Scapa Flow in Orkney, Scotland, where eight German ships were scuttled in 1919, to Plymouth's HMS *Scylla*, which was purposely sunk in 2004 to create an artificial reef.

Marine life in the UK is as diverse as it is wonderful. You can dive with seals and basking sharks, explore reefs with their myriad fish or marvel at ornate soft corals or kelp forests. And given the right training, experience, equipment and conditions, the seas around our coast are accessible all year round.

Have a go...

If you have never tried scuba before, then I'd recommend starting with a 'try dive' with your local British Sub-Aqua Club (www.bsac.com), or with your local PADI Dive Centre (www.padi.co.uk). All the basics are covered – from your scuba kit to techniques needed to breathe under water for the very first time. And you are taught everything in the safe environment of your local swimming pool (BSAC has over 1,000 local branches). For true enthusiasts, the BSAC entry-level Ocean Diver course (designed for complete beginners) will enable you to dive to a maximum depth of 20 metres and check out the UK's (and if you like, the world's) best diving spots.

Voted top of the spots*

★ SCAPA FLOW, Orkney
★ FARNE ISLANDS, Northumberland
★ PLYMOUTH SOUND
★ ST ABBS, Berwickshire
★ SOUND OF MULL
★ OBAN
★ CORNWALL
★ WEYMOUTH
★ JAMES EGAN LANE (wreck off coast of Plymouth)

* in a recent BSAC member survey

Sleeping out under the stars

This is when it all starts to get a bit magical. We haven't slept in the open, under the stars very often but when we have it's been wonderful. The last time we did it in style, with a futon and a duvet. The stars were bright, because there was no light pollution to spoil the view, and all we could hear was the crack and snap of a small summer swell. We should do it more often.

WHAT'S ABOVE?

I'm no astronomer. But what I do know is that the night sky is, and should be, full of wonder. It should inspire you to ask questions. It should make you feel small. Once upon a time (in the dark days before iPhones) our kind navigated, told the time and lived out dreams through celestial events. Our language is peppered with astral references. Nowadays, of course, we live in boxes and under streetlights, so it's not so easy to be guided by the heavens. But when we are in the countryside where there is no light pollution, no cloud of haze and nothing to distract us, we should take the opportunity to look up once in a while. It's worth it.

Stargazing tips
* Summer is a good time to stargaze.
* Stargazing can hurt your neck. So get a blanket and lie on your back. You'll get a better view.
* Nights when there is no moon will be best for stargazing.
* Places where there is no light pollution will also be best.
* Using a pair of binoculars can really begin to bring the night sky alive.

SEASIDE SECRETS: Have you ever wondered what stars are above your head, and when? Do you know their names or which constellation they belong to? Well, for about £8 you will be able to unlock the mysteries of the universe with a very simple but clever device called a Planisphere. It's a circular dial which will show you what is where in the night sky on the day you are looking. It's very clever. We keep one in the van. Takes up no space at all.

Look out for

★ Manmade satellites/aircraft/falling space junk, which burn as a green fireball.

★ The Seven Sisters, found in the star cluster Pleiades.

★ Single and double ice rings around the moon, best seen in the autumn.

★ Noctilucent or night clouds. A beautiful pale blue streak or whirl across the sky, best illuminated by the sun when it's dipped below the horizon, just after a good sunset.

★ Lunar eclipses – more common than you might think.

★ The awe-inspiring Milky Way. Our home galaxy stretches across the night sky. 100,000,000 light years across, it contains billions of stars.

★ The planet Venus, often visible near where the sun has just set.

★ The four Galilean moons of Jupiter – Io, Europa, Ganymede and Callisto.

★ Meteor showers – like shooting stars, eclipses and comets, meteor showers are the superstars of the night sky. Simply put, they occur when bits and bobs of space dust and particles burn up in the Earth's atmosphere. The Perseids is one of the best to observe. Look towards the north-east after midnight, around 13th and 14th August, for this all-singing, all-dancing heavenward happening.

Festival season

GET THAT FESTIVAL FEELING

Festivals are big business these days. And there are all types of things going
on. Usually they involve people gathering to do something, see something or be
something. I'm all for them, although the atmosphere can vary enormously between
events (see page 152 for my favourites). Which is why it's wise to choose carefully
which ones to attend.

COASTAL VW FESTIVALS

Even in the VW world, each festival is unique. Some are massive, some are aimed at families and some are just like a weekend camping with your mates. The great thing is that anything goes, unless the teens get hold of the vodka, in which case it's time to go to bed. Surprisingly there aren't many VW shows on the coast, but here is a handful where you can get really close ...

VANWEST takes place in the caravan-park hell of Somerset's coast. But it is a great little show and a drive on the beach at Brean will make the weekend truly memorable. Weston Super Mare, May.

RUN TO THE SUN is what everyone thinks of when they think VW festival. And rightly so. A cruise from Reading Services to Newquay, then a great big party. Whoopee! Although it might not be sunny. Newquay, May.

VANTASTIVAL is a big old friendly hoo-ha that sees VW owners from all over Ireland converge in a field to eat, drink and be merry. I loved it. Dunany, Co. Louth, May.

MIGHTY DUB FEST is on the beach in Northumberland. Watersports and campers? Fan-dub-tastic! Druridge Bay, Northumberland, June.

DUBS AT THE CASTLE is a little further from the sea but I'm including it because the guys who organise it rock. That is all. Caldicott, Wales, July.

BEACHBUGGIN' takes place in Southsea, Hants. It's been going for ages and is right on the seafront. Southsea, Hampshire, August.

BRIGHTON BREEZE is a classic cruise that leaves London for the seaside at Brighton. Loved by all and ends up with a gathering on the seafront. London-Brighton, October.

fiery festival falafels with
ROCKET AND MINTY YOGHURT

Even if you don't get to a festival this year, these will put you right in the mood. Fry 'em up, put some mud on your wellies, turn up the radio and stand in the rain. Yeah man. Sorted.

◀ FOR 4

400G TIN CHICKPEAS

3 OR 4 SPRING ONIONS, FINELY CHOPPED

1 HEAPED TBSP FINELY CHOPPED CORIANDER

1 HEAPED TBSP FINELY CHOPPED PARSLEY

1 SMALL RED CHILLI, DESEEDED AND FINELY CHOPPED

2 CLOVES GARLIC, FINELY CHOPPED

1 TSP CUMIN

1 TSP SESAME SEEDS

SQUEEZE OF LEMON JUICE

1 LARGE EGG

PLAIN FLOUR, FOR DUSTING

VEGETABLE OIL, FOR FRYING

4 PITTA BREADS

2 HANDFULS ROCKET

FOR THE MINTY YOGHURT

150MLS NATURAL YOGHURT

1 HEAPED TBSP FINELY CHOPPED MINT

5 CM PIECE CUCUMBER, DICED

SQUEEZE OF LEMON JUICE

For the falafel mixture, drain the tin of chickpeas, then tip the chickpeas into a mixing bowl and mash them with the back of a fork or a potato masher. Mix in the chopped spring onions, herbs, chilli, garlic, cumin, sesame seeds, lemon juice and some seasoning. Next crack the egg into the mixture and stir to combine thoroughly. Cover and leave for about half an hour in a cool place (in the fridge, if it's on) to firm up. Meanwhile, make the minty yoghurt by mixing all the ingredients together.

To form the falafels, flour your hands and spoon a heaped teaspoon of the mixture into them, then roll it into a ball. Dust with a little extra flour, set aside. Repeat with the rest of the mixture – it's a bit messy, but worth it and you should end up with about 16 falafel balls.

Next, heat up a frying pan with about ½ cm of vegetable oil. Fry the falafels for 5 minutes or until they are crispy all over. Keep them moving, as they cook, to maintain their shape. Grill the pitta breads on both sides. Fill each pitta with rocket and four falafel and drizzle with the minty yoghurt.

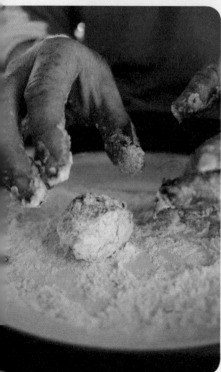

YOUR OWN PRIVATE FUNSTOCK

Of course you can have a festival of your own, wherever you go. You don't have to have live music or famous bands or helicopters bringing posh guests on to your campsite. Just two people can make a festival, although it might be at the more 'acoustic' end of the festival spectrum. Strictly speaking, you don't even have to hold your gathering in a muddy field, although all the best jokes about UK festivals will involve that sooner or later. I say, do it down at the beach or somewhere you can camp within sight of the water.

The rules

★ Have a good festival name and make sure this name ends in -stock or -fest. We've had Vanstock, Dubstock, Vanfest and even Woodstock. My friends Dave and Jen hold Crapstock on their farm every year. You get the picture?

★ Make a focus for your evening's entertainment. This could be a gazebo or a good place to watch the sun go down or just a fire on the beach.

★ If you've got electricity, take fairy lights. If you haven't, bring lots of tea candles, jam jars and vintage fabrics for a lovely twilight effect.

★ Make fancy dress compulsory for Saturday night. Even if there are just four of you.

★ Bunting is a must. And cute kids in PJs and wellies add a lovely family vibe.

★ Create an area reserved for glamping. That way you can persuade your posh friends to come. But don't do anything special for them, just make it nearer the toilet.

★ Don't be cool about music. Go for something that's classic, retro and fun and will get you in the mood for good times.

★ Bring wellies. Ha ha. No, seriously. Bring wellies.

There are some tastes that are unmistakable. Some simply scream of the summer don't they? Chicken and tarragon, paella, ratatouille, lamb and mint. And these are the recipes that will make it happen.

new potatoes with hazelnuts,
MUSHROOMS AND CRUNCH

The first new potatoes are an early summer treat that shouldn't be missed. If you can get wild mushrooms or are happy to forage for them (you might find chanterelles or field mushrooms if you are lucky) and know what you are doing, they will add a special something to this dish. The radishes add crunch and freshness.

FOR 2, OR 3 AS A SIDE
GENEROUS DOUBLE HANDFUL SMALLISH NEW POTATOES
OLIVE OIL
2-3 TBSP SHELLED HAZELNUTS
2 HANDFULS MUSHROOMS, HALVED OR SLICED
8 RADISHES

Halve or quarter the potatoes, depending on size, then simmer them in salted water for about 10 minutes or until really tender.

Meanwhile, heat a tablespoon of oil in a frying pan and roughly chop the hazelnuts. Toast the chopped hazelnuts in the oil with a pinch of salt for a few minutes until golden. Tip onto a plate. Next fry the mushrooms, in the same pan, until tender, a matter of minutes. Trim and slice the radishes.

Drain the potatoes, return them to the pan and press on each one with the back of a fork to smash them. Add the hazelnuts, mushrooms, a decent slug of olive oil and some seasoning. Toss everything together over the heat. Add the radishes, toss again and pile onto plates.

canarian seawater spuds
WITH A GREEN MOJO DIP

If you like garlic, then this is for you. It's a great way to cook spuds that's kinda simple yet absolutely beautiful. It's the most effective way of using seawater that I've ever come across, because of the gorgeous, salt-encrusted potatoes that the process creates. We've had this dish in the Canaries, where they serve it at every opportunity.

◀ FOR 4, AS A STARTER OR ACCOMPANIMENT TO MEAT OR FISH DISHES
1KG SMALL POTATOES

FOR THE MOJO DIP
HALF A SMALL BULB OF GARLIC, FINELY CHOPPED
½ TSP SALT
2 GOOD PINCHES GROUND CUMIN
3 TBSP FINELY CHOPPED CORIANDER
100MLS VEGETABLE OIL
3-4 TBSP WHITE WINE VINEGAR

Boil the potatoes in clean seawater (or heavily salted water, see below) for 15 to 20 minutes. It pays a little to overcook the spuds slightly as they will wrinkle better later.

Meanwhile, make the mojo dip. Crush the chopped garlic to a paste in a pestle and mortar with the salt and cumin. Add the coriander and pound together. Gradually add the oil, mixing all the time. Finally add enough vinegar to make the dip the consistency you like. When the spuds are cooked, drain away the water then put the pan back on the stove over a gentle flame. The remaining water will evaporate from the skins of the spuds and the skins will wrinkle. Salt will begin to crystallise on the surface. Serve when the water has completely evaporated. Dip them into the mojo as you eat. If you don't have access to fresh seawater dissolve enough salt in a pan of water to make a potato float.

FOR A VARIATION
For a red mojo dip, use 3 red chillies, deseeded and chopped, instead of the garlic, add half a teaspoon of hot paprika and leave out the coriander.

RATATOUILLE

This will make a fine main course or a great accompaniment for lamb or fish. You can also try it tossed with capers, cooked penne and lots of grated Parmesan.

FOR 4, OR 6 AS A SIDE
OLIVE OIL, FOR FRYING
2 ONIONS, CHOPPED
6 RIPE, MEDIUM TOMATOES (WELL-FLAVOURED IS BEST)
2 RED PEPPERS
2 COURGETTES
1 SMALLISH AUBERGINE
2 CLOVES GARLIC, CRUSHED
PINCH OF SUGAR
FEW SPRIGS THYME
SMALL HANDFUL BASIL LEAVES, TORN

Heat 3 tablespoons of olive oil in a medium-sized pan and cook the onions for 8-10 minutes: you don't want them to brown, just to soften, slowly. Boil a kettle of water.

Put the tomatoes in a bowl and pour boiling water over them. Leave for 30 seconds, then drain, peel, halve and deseed – discard the seeds and chop the flesh. Halve, deseed and chop the peppers into smallish chunks. Trim the courgettes, halve them lengthways and chop. Trim and chop the aubergine. You want all the vegetables to be roughly the same size.

Stir the tomato flesh, crushed garlic, sugar and thyme into the softened onions. Gently simmer, uncovered, for 10 minutes, stirring. In a frying pan, cook the peppers, courgettes and aubergines in oil, in batches, until soft and tinged brown.

Fish out and discard the thyme from the tomatoes and add the fried vegetables. Season and stir to mix, then bubble together for 5 minutes or so – add a couple of tablespoons of water if needed. Finally stir in the basil – eat warm rather than piping hot so all the flavours shine.

fisherman's salad
WITH SUMMER SALSA

FOR 4

1 SMALL BULB FENNEL

HALF A CUCUMBER

JUICE OF HALF A LEMON

3 TBSP OLIVE OIL

FEW PINCHES OF FENNEL SEED

8 FISH FILLETS

8 SCALLOPS OR 2 HANDFULS RAW PRAWNS

4 BIG HANDFULS MIXED SALAD LEAVES

SEASONED FLOUR, OIL AND BUTTER

FOR THE SUMMER SALSA

4 RIPE TOMATOES

1 SMALL CLOVE GARLIC, FINELY CHOPPED

4 TBSP OLIVE OIL

3 TBSP CHOPPED HERBS, 1 EACH OF
  TARRAGON, MINT, AND BASIL OR PARSLEY

SQUEEZE OF LEMON JUICE

PINCH OF SUGAR

SEA SALT FLAKES

Trim and finely slice the fennel. Peel the cucumber and slice into batons, then mix in a large bowl with the fennel, lemon juice, olive oil and the fennel seed, then set aside.

For the salsa, put the tomatoes into a bowl, cover with boiling water and leave for a minute, then drain and peel. Halve the tomatoes, scoop out and discard the seeds, chop the flesh. In a smallish bowl, mix the flesh with the garlic, olive oil, herbs, lemon juice and a pinch each of sugar and salt.

Now, cook your catch (or buy) – dust fish fillets with seasoned flour and fry, in batches, in a little oil and butter for a few minutes on each side. Scallops or prawns will take a minute, or less, on each side so wipe out the pan and fry them afterwards over a highish heat until golden and cooked through.

Toss the mixed leaves with the fennel salad and some seasoning. Eat with the seafood and salsa.

joanne's cally chicken
WITH TARRAGON AND LEMON

Oh California! How we love you. Or, more to the point, how Joanne loved her camping and hostelling trip to California some time in the years BM (before Martin). As well as The Boyfriend Potato Salad (that I jealously named after her all-American ex-boy, Brad) that featured in *The Camper Van Cookbook*, she also picked up another recipe, Cally Chicken. This one is easy and versatile and perfectly delicious on a hot summer's day. It is simple enough to be cooked by a tipsy Irish girl in California on a camping stove in Yosemite National Park and if that's possible, you can do it too.

◀ FOR 2

1 COURGETTE

2 CHICKEN BREASTS

OLIVE OIL, FOR FRYING

6 CHERRY TOMATOES

1 GLASS WHITE WINE

JUICE OF 2 LEMONS AND THE ZEST OF 1

SMALL HANDFUL TARRAGON LEAVES, TORN

GREEN SALAD LEAVES AND BREAD, TO SERVE

First trim the courgette and then slice it – into rings or thinly lengthways. Next dice the chicken and heat a splash of olive oil in a frying pan. Fry the chicken pieces for 5 minutes, turning regularly. At the same time, cut each tomato into four.

Pour the white wine into the pan and let that bubble away for a minute or so. Next add the lemon juice, the tarragon, the tomatoes and the courgette slices.

Cook and stir together over a medium heat for a further 5 minutes. Serve with the green salad leaves, using the sauce as a dressing. Sprinkle everything with lemon zest before enjoying with crusty bread.

one pan lamb with peas,
BROAD BEANS AND MINT

If the sun is shining, cook the lamb on a moderately hot barbecue. It will take
12-15 minutes.

FOR 4
2 SPRING ONIONS
LARGE KNOB BUTTER
4 HANDFULS SHELLED PEAS
3 HANDFULS SHELLED SMALL BROAD BEANS
200MLS VEGETABLE OR CHICKEN STOCK
OIL FOR FRYING
2 TRIMMED, SKIN-ON, BONELESS LAMB LOIN FILLETS, EACH ABOUT 230G
2 TBSP SHREDDED MINT

Trim and slice the spring onions. Heat half of the butter in a frying pan until foaming. Fry
the spring onions for a few minutes, to soften. Stir in the peas, broad beans and stock.
Bring everything to simmering point and simmer rapidly, uncovered, for 3-4 minutes
or till the beans and peas are tender and most of the stock has evaporated. Tip into a
bowl.

Add the rest of the butter and a spot of oil to the pan and when sizzling, cook the
lamb fillets over a medium to high heat for 5 minutes on each side. Then, stand the
fillets onto one of their longer edges and cook for a couple of minutes before doing the
same with the other side, so you end up with fillets that are golden all over but still pink
in the middle. Remove them from the pan onto a plate.

Drain the fat from the pan and return the bean mixture to it. Add the mint and some
seasoning and stir over the heat to warm through. Slice the lamb, arrange on top of the
beans and peas and serve from the pan.

camper van PAELLA

Whilst you might not carry a paella dish in your camper van, they are handy things to have around. You can use them for all kinds of stuff and they don't weigh much. Stash one at the bottom of the cupboard and forget about it until the time comes for the paella party. Light up a fire and go for it (let's face it, you'll have to as your dish will never fit on your stove).

FOR 4

8 LARGE SHELL-ON RAW MEDITERRANEAN PRAWNS (CREVETTES)

2 GENEROUS PINCHES SAFFRON

OIL, FOR FRYING

4 SKIN-ON CHICKEN THIGHS (OR SAME QUANTITY RABBIT)

A HANDFUL CHOPPED CHORIZO

1 ONION, FINELY CHOPPED

1 CLOVE GARLIC, FINELY CHOPPED

1 RED PEPPER, DESEEDED AND CHOPPED

250MLS BOMBA PAELLA RICE

½ TSP SMOKED PAPRIKA

2 HANDFULS MUSSELS, SCRUBBED AND BEARDS REMOVED

SMALL BUNCH OF PARSLEY, CHOPPED

WEDGES OF LEMON, TO SERVE

Shell the prawns, leaving their tails intact and put the shells and heads in a medium pan with 3 mugfuls (850mls) of cold water. Bring to the boil, then reduce the heat to low and leave the stock to simmer for 20 minutes. Put the saffron into a mug and add 1 tablespoon boiling water to soak.

When the stock is ready, strain it and discard the prawn heads and shells. Heat a tablespoon of oil in a large shallow-sided pan and fry the chicken over a medium heat for 12-15 minutes, turning, until golden all over. Remove from the pan and discard the fat. Brown the chorizo in the pan, transfer to a plate.

Now fry the onion for 5 minutes, until browned. Add the garlic and red pepper and cook, stirring, for a couple of minutes.

Tip the rice into the pan along with the saffron and its liquid, the paprika, chorizo and some seasoning, stir. Add two mugfuls of the strained stock and more or less submerge the chicken in the rice and liquid. Bring the stock to simmering point, then leave the paella to gently bubble away, uncovered, for 10 minutes, adding extra stock if needed.

Push the prawns into the rice and scatter the mussels on top, cover and leave the paella over a gentle heat for 10 minutes, so any remaining stock is absorbed and the prawns and mussels cook – turn the prawns over halfway and discard any mussels that don't open. Sprinkle with parsley, serve with lemon wedges.

Tener una buena noche!

poached greengages or apricots
WITH LEMON AND LIME CREAM

This recipe is good for fruit that isn't perfectly ripe. It makes a simple pud that's perfect for a crowd. Taste the fruit and add sugar to cook it in accordingly. If the fruit is ripe it may only need a couple of tablespoonfuls.

FOR 8
300MLS DOUBLE CREAM
5-6 TBSP CASTER SUGAR
JUICE OF HALF A LEMON AND A LIME
16-24 GREENGAGES OR APRICOTS
5-6 TBSP ELDERFLOWER CORDIAL

169
SUMMER

Gently heat the cream with 3 tablespoons of the sugar in a medium-sized pan and once the sugar has dissolved, turn the heat up and boil the mixture for 3 minutes exactly. Then, remove the pan from the heat and stir in the lemon and lime juice. Tip the mixture into a bowl and leave to cool and set, then chill (if the fridge is working).

Halve and stone the greengages or apricots and put into a pan with the rest of the sugar, the elderflower cordial and a couple of tablespoonfuls of water. Gently mix.

Bring the liquid to simmering point, then cover the pan and simmer for 5-6 minutes or until the fruit is soft but not losing its shape – the time will depend on its ripeness. Cool. Eat the poached fruit with the citrus cream.

strawberry 'MESS'

It's summer right? Well you can't have summer without strawberries. And you can't have a summer camping trip without a 'mess'. For a variation, turn into strawberry shortcakes – just replace the meringue with crumbled shortbread biscuits.

FOR 4

16 STRAWBERRIES

2 TBSP ICING SUGAR

150MLS DOUBLE OR WHIPPING CREAM

½ VANILLA POD, SPLIT LENGTHWAYS AND SEEDS REMOVED, OR DASH
  OF VANILLA EXTRACT (NOT ESSENTIAL)

3 TBSP GREEK YOGHURT

2 INDIVIDUAL MERINGUE NESTS

Wash, hull and roughly chop the strawberries, and mix them in a bowl with the icing sugar.

In a second bowl whip the cream with the vanilla seeds or extract until just forming soft peaks, then mix with the yoghurt.

Put a layer of strawberries with their juice into four cups (or glasses) – use about three quarters of the strawberries. Add the meringues to the yoghurt mixture, breaking them into small chunks as you do so. Top the strawberries in the cups with the yoghurt mixture, followed by the remaining strawberries. Eat as soon as possible before the meringue dissolves.

strawberries and raspberries
WITH ZESTY SUGAR

A fresh and fruity treat. Eat this with thick yoghurt or whipped cream.

FOR 4

20 STRAWBERRIES

ZEST OF AN ORANGE (OR LEMON)

2 TBSP CASTER SUGAR

SMALL HANDFUL SHREDDED BASIL (OR HALF THE QUANTITY OF MINT)

3 HANDFULS (250G) RASPBERRIES

Hull and slice the strawberries. Mix the zest, sugar and basil. Toss with the strawberries and raspberries and leave to macerate for 15-20 minutes.

A TEA FOR SUMMER: organic, fresh peppermint tea

Mint grows wild on some coastal landscapes, so if you see it, pick it. It aids the digestion of food and can soothe upset stomachs. Didn't you ever wonder why the after-dinner mint was so popular? Plus, peppermint can relax muscles, so it's perfect for a post-surf tisane. Choose a few blemish-free leaves, wash and tear them up slightly, to help release the beneficial oils.

MAKING THE PERFECT CUPPA

The Tea Appreciation Society recommends using a glass teapot with an in-built filter or a cafetière, but don't worry if you don't have them aboard. (Glass teapot? In a camper van? Whatever next?) A clean melamine mug will do just as well. Use boiled water (but not on the boil), then, when the tea is brewed to your liking, spoon out the leaves. Peppermint shouldn't need sweetening but if you must add sugar, I'm not telling. Honey would work too.

Autumn

Plentiful seas and frosty mornings

Some people can't get to grips with autumn. In theory, if you've enjoyed a long summer at the coast then the return to work and school would make the day after the last day of the holidays a little bit like the worst Monday morning ever. I remember that feeling. But not here, my all-weather friends!

For us, the autumn means a return to normality after the madness of the summer. We do our best to eke out the last few drops of golden sunshine – and often with spectacular results. The sea is at its warmest and won't begin to cool down properly until the first wintry storms in November, so we can still enjoy a day at the beach with buckets and spades and smiles. My feet, feeling cold walking down the beach for an early morning surf session, find a steaming, late year Atlantic oddly warming. On the east coast, of course, the booties come on sooner.

Autumn is the time for change. It's when the dewy mornings and starry skies meet the winds of the west and the downpours of the Gulf Stream. One minute you could be fishing, the next running for cover. But throw in a few extra togs, dig out the winter woollies and get on with enjoying the harvest before it's too late.

Who could ever forget the joy of blackberry picking, of returning to base camp with juice-stained faces? It's one of the few times when we'll all feel confident out in the wilds. But they also grow side by side with mushrooms and elderberries, if you have the nerve (and a very good field guide to show you the way). A walk along the coast path will reward you with stunted, low-growing sloes too. Fill your pockets while you can.

Shellfish are back on the menu come the low spring tides of autumn. More moules? Yes please. Further out, the pelagic hordes of mackerel and herring hang about in search of a few shimmering sprats to gorge on before winter. If you're lucky, you'll see the sea splash and boil with joyful gluttony as they make chase towards the high tide mark. I'll be there, with my rod and bucket, ever hopeful, sometimes lucky, never downhearted.

Especially in times of plenty.

Autumn we love you.

Autumn fishing

It is the warm water that brings them, the mackerel. All year they stay offshore, in enormous shoals, waiting for the day when the water warms up enough for them to head inshore and gobble up the small fry. Late summer and early autumn is prime time for them in our neck of the woods as the water is at its warmest all year. On odd days you'll see the water boiling with them as they chase the baby sprats and herring up the coast. Sometimes you'll find a shimmering silver carpet of beached whitebait on the shore. If you do, scoop them up in a net and take them home for tea. Nothing like a few small fry rolled in flour and chilli flakes and fried up in butter and olive oil.

This is the time of year when everyone on our coast becomes a fisherman because it's now that a trip to your local pier or sea wall will usually yield a result of some kind. The experienced go for bass, whilst the novices and idiots (like me) stay happy with a haul of mackerel for the pot.

THE BRAINY OPTION

As long as you catch mackerel yourself or buy it line-caught, then you are buying one of the most sustainable fish available. Plus, it is full of omega-3 so it is regularly classed as brain food. Whether or not it will actually make you more cleverer is up for debate. Lastly, mackerel tastes brilliant and is very versatile. I'd like to think that I am a mackerel champion because of the environment but really it's because it's the only fish I ever manage to catch. I suppose that says it all though, doesn't it?

OFF-SHORE FISHING

Instead of tangling lines with all the other autumn amateurs, why not...

PADDLE OUT ON YOUR SURFBOARD. Trust me when I say that it's much easier if you take a hand line with you rather than a rod. From experience I can say that it is, in fact, near impossible to thread a rod that's longer than your surfboard when you are trying to sit on your surfboard. Attach the hand line to your person and paddle along with it. Stealthily position yourself above where the fishes live. Use a set of feathers or a brightly coloured spinner. Mackerel love it. (See page 144 for more on SUP.)

PADDLE OUT ON YOUR KAYAK. If you have one, this is the way to do it. You'll cover plenty of ground and will be able to troll as you head out towards the shoals (look for bird activity). Once you're in the spot, you can cast from the canoe. Sooner or later you're bound to find a fish at the end of the line. When you hit a secluded bay you can cook it for your tea. What more could you ask?

HIRE A BOAT AND SKIPPER. With the benefit of a fish finder you'll never be short of a few mackers for the barbie. They might even be able to get you 'something else'. Imagine! This is the easy way to do it. Mind you, there's still no guarantee, even with the best skipper in the world. We had a skipper once who swore blind we'd get bass. I hooked a mackerel but he lost it when he tried to land it for me. He shouted at other boats.

Make your own hand line

This is easy. You can buy fishing line from any fishing tackle shop. All you need is:

LINE. With the breaking strain of a few pounds (unless you intend to fish for shark).

A SET OF FEATHERS. This is a line of hooks with feathers attached. Mackerel love them.

A LEAD WEIGHT. This will take the line to the bottom. If you intend to troll for mackerel from a surfboard or kayak don't make it too light.

A HANDLE OF SOME DESCRIPTION. The handle of a kite or even a bottle will do for this, so long as you can safely wrap the line around it, without it coming off.

THE EASY WAY TO GUT A MACKEREL

I was taught this trick by my friend Chris Braund the fisherman. He's got proper mutton-chop side burns and everything and knows how to do stuff with boats and fish that most of us (and by that I mean me) don't. So. Grab your mackerel in your left hand and, with a very sharp knife and without cutting yourself, make a cut in the back of the mackerel's head (just above the gills) and through the spine. Then pull the head downwards and back towards the tail. The head should come off and with it the entrails, leaving a nice cavity, which can then be easily cleaned.

HOW TO FILLET A MACKEREL

With the palm of your hand hold the gutted mackerel firmly on a board. Then, with a filleting knife, cut from the tail along the backbone. This should release the fillet. Trim off the fins. Turn over and do the same on the other side.

Freshly caught mackerel is a rare treat and if spanking fresh it is delicious eaten as sashimi, drizzled with soy sauce with some wasabi and pickled ginger alongside. Here are a few other ideas

mackerel with a
VIETNAMESE DRESSING

FOR 2

JUICE OF A FAT LIME

1 RED OR GREEN CHILLI, DESEEDED AND FINELY DICED

2 TSP CASTER SUGAR

1 TBSP RICE VINEGAR

2 TBSP CHOPPED CORIANDER

1 TBSP CHOPPED MINT

OIL, FOR FRYING

SMALL HANDFUL NATURAL ROASTED PEANUTS

2 TBSP PLAIN FLOUR

4 MACKEREL FILLETS

In a bowl mix the first six ingredients with a pinch of salt to make a dressing.

Heat a couple of tablespoons of oil in a frying pan. Toast the peanuts in the hot oil for 3-4 minutes or till golden, drain on kitchen paper and set aside (discard the oil). Scatter the flour onto a plate, mix with a little salt.

Re-heat the frying pan with a tablespoon of oil. Dip the fillets, one by one, in the flour, shaking off any excess and then fry in the hot oil in the frying pan for 3-4 minutes on each side or till crispy and cooked through. Roughly chop the peanuts.

Transfer the fish to plates, drizzle with the Vietnamese dressing and scatter with the peanuts. Eat straight away.

mackerel with
MUSTARD CAPER BUTTER

FOR 2

2 TBSP SOFT UNSALTED BUTTER
1 ROUNDED TSP DIJON OR GRAINY MUSTARD
1 TSP SMALL CAPERS
4 MACKEREL FILLETS

In a bowl, mix the butter, mustard and capers.

Grill the mackerel fillets, flesh side up, for 4 minutes. Dot the fillets with the butter and then grill for a further 2-3 minutes or till the butter is melted and bubbling.

mackerel with tomatoes,
CHORIZO AND FENNEL SEED

FOR 2

4 TBSP CHOPPED CHORIZO
4 RIPE, MEDIUM TOMATOES, CHOPPED
2 TSP FENNEL SEED
4 MACKEREL FILLETS
1-2 TBSP CHOPPED PARSLEY

Preheat the grill.

Fry the chorizo, in a frying pan and in its own fat, till browned. Add the tomatoes and fennel seed and a pinch of salt. Simmer together for 5 minutes, stirring occasionally – the tomatoes will cook down and you will end up with a sauce of sorts; add a dash of water if necessary.

Grill the mackerel fillets, flesh side up, for 5-6 minutes or till cooked through. Top with the sauce and finish with a scattering of parsley.

mackerel with miso, SOY AND SESAME

FOR 2

10G SACHET INSTANT MISO SOUP

2 TSP SESAME OIL

2 TSP SOY SAUCE

1 TBSP RUNNY HONEY

1 TBSP SESAME SEEDS

2 SPRING ONIONS, CHOPPED

4 MACKEREL FILLETS

Preheat the grill.

In a bowl, mix the miso soup powder, the oil, soy sauce and honey with a teaspoon of water. Toast the sesame seeds in a frying pan over a medium heat, tip into a bowl. Trim and finely chop the spring onions.

Line a baking tray with foil and place the mackerel fillets on it, side by side, flesh side up. Spoon the miso mixture over the mackerel. Grill for 5-6 minutes or till cooked through, basting the mackerel halfway. Scatter with the spring onions and toasted sesame seeds.

mackerel in NEWSPAPER

◄ You want an easy way to cook a mackerel? This is it. And it works too.

First, catch a mackerel. Next, gut it (see page 177) and stuff it with herbs, a slice of lemon and seasoning. Then wrap it in a sheet of newspaper and soak the newspaper thoroughly with fresh water. Repeat this five times until you have a wet mackerel parcel. Now place it on a barbecue or an open fire and cook it until it starts to burn the paper, almost to the point at which it catches fire.

The moisture in the water will keep the fish from burning long enough to allow it to steam in its own juices. Once you unwrap it, the fish will be perfectly cooked. Serve it up with our 'camper van chips' (page 141).

Got fish? Smoke it!
A recipe for easy in-van smoking

I had always assumed that smoking fish (or smoking any kind of food for that matter) was seriously complicated, involving all kinds of post-industrial cast-offs, tubes and tins to build a gurgling and smouldering something that growled and coughed every time you walked past. But no. Smoking, it seems, can be quick and easy and very tasty and there are ways of doing it that are both easy and portable.

Hot smoking is all about salt, moisture, smoke and heat. The tricky bit is getting the combination right in the traditional way. In Arbroath, it's an art that has been refined over generations so that genuine Arbroath Smokies have just the right flavour. If you get the chance to try one hot off the barrel, do. They are sensational. In fact, tasting one, on the beach in Auchmithie in eastern Scotland (the place where they were invented), fired up my taste buds in search of a 'camper van way'. Thanks to my friend Alyson at Hot Smoked, I found it.

PORTABLE HOT SMOKERS

The one I have is like an oversized sardine tin – about 10" long by 6" wide by 3" deep – and it is easily stored in the van, out of sight. It consists of a tin box with sliding lid, a drip tray and a wire rack. The day I got one, it revolutionised my food capabilities and opened my eyes to a whole new way of cooking.

You can really add to your outdoor repertoire. Mussels straight off the beach? Easy peasy. Chuck your smoker in your rucksack, pick a few big 'uns at low tide, make a fire, smoke them for 10 minutes. They will steam in their own juices, then, when the shells open, the smoke will infuse the flesh with a delightfully deep oakiness. It's powerful stuff.

To make your hot smoker work, all you need is a heat source and some wood dust to smoke with. A tablespoon of oak dust will do it. Place it under the drip tray, load the wire rack with fresh mackerel (or whatever), season, chuck it on a fire and wait for 10 minutes. Bingo! Hot smoked mackerel that tastes like nothing you've ever tasted before, I promise.

It doesn't stop there. Portable hot smokers steam the food as well as smoke it because of the heat. That means you can add a little water to the drip tray to help the steaming process. In fact, you can add just about anything. I've cooked a duck breast with orange zest, red wine and garlic in the drip tray. It works too.

The other thing you can do is to alter the type of wood dust you use. You can buy all types and each will give you a slightly different flavour. Fruit woods such as apple will add another dimension to the taste. Salting before smoking helps to draw out the moisture in the flesh, which also helps the flesh to take on the smoke flavours. If you like experimenting, then this is for you. Eventually you'll happen upon a combination of salt, smoke and fish (or meat) that will blow your mind. You can also play about with herb rubs – again these will add new depths and layers to the flavours. The possibilities are endless.

Make your own smoker

You can buy smokers, dust and rubs from www.hotsmoked.co.uk. Or you can make your own with just a few simple items, experimenting along the way until you get it right. You'll need:

ONE OLD BISCUIT TIN (check your mum has finished with it first)
ONE OLD BISCUIT TIN LID (slightly smaller than the first one preferably)
SOME CHICKEN WIRE (or a cake rack that fits your biscuit tin)
SOME WOOD DUST (don't sweep the workshop floor, buy it. Or at least make sure it's a hard wood and is very clean before you use it)

Place the lid inside the tin so that it forms a drip tray, make a wire rack inside with the chicken wire, make a few small holes in the lid and then off you go. It's simplicity itself (and just the way I like it). To use, place it on a heat source and allow it to heat up enough to make the wood dust smoulder. Use a medium to high heat.

easy smoked mackerel pâté
ON TOAST WITH RADISHES

Once you've got to grips with your portable smoker you'll have so much smoked mackerel that you won't know what to do with it. So why not put it to good use and make this simple and delicious pâté?

◀ FOR 2

6 SLICES FROM A BAGUETTE
2 FILLETS SMOKED MACKEREL
4 TBSP CREAM CHEESE
1 TBSP CAPERS
A SMALL SQUEEZE OF LEMON JUICE, PLUS THE ZEST OF A LEMON
OLIVE OIL
2 RADISHES, SLICED

Preheat the grill on a low setting. Slowly toast the baguette slices on both sides until they are golden and really crispy.

Remove the bones and skin from the mackerel fillets and mash the fish in a bowl with the cream cheese, capers and the lemon juice.

When the slices of toast are ready, drizzle them with olive oil (you could even rub them with a cut garlic clove too, if you fancy). Spread pâté onto the toasts and finish each one with a slice or two of radish and a sprinkling of lemon zest.

Catch your own shellfish supper

There's so much that can be eaten along the seashore. From mussels to seaweeds, it's all there for the taking – as long as you have permission. Much like any other type of fishing, catching seafood is a bit of a game and can require some stealthy means, especially if you want to catch crabs, shrimps, prawns and lobster. Mind you, if you want an easy life, go for slower, less desirable creatures like winkles, mussels or limpets. You can eat them all and they can't run away or nip you in the same way that a crab can. Happy hunting.

PUTTING OUT A TRAP FOR LATER

Despite a few years of putting out traps, I have never caught the lobster that I wanted. But I have caught edible (common or brown) crabs, lots of terrifying, mad-eyed velvet swimmer crabs and a couple of dog fish. It's a scary thing to put your hand into a trap to pull out what is essentially a very fed up mini-shark.

You can buy traps in all shapes and sizes and they can be used to catch all kinds of thing. Apparently. Creels and traps can only be put out (without a boat) at low tide and low autumn tides are by far the best times. With warmer water at this time of the year there will be plenty of creatures close to the shore eager to take the bait. Collapsible traps are really easy to use and usually come with two one-way entrances that crabs, fish and shrimps can crawl into to get at the bait you leave for them.

As with all alternative fishing methods, pots are covered by local fishing by-laws, governing where and when you can use them and what kind of pots are allowed. In my area, for example, you cannot use certain types of pots with inner chambers unless they have an escape gap to allow undersized lobster and crab to escape. The people at the Sea Fisheries are very helpful and will answer any questions you have about setting traps and pots. You can buy your traps and creels at www.castnets.co.uk.

WHAT'S IN THE POT?

If you are very lucky you might find a brown crab. If you do and it's more than 160 mm across the back of its shell then it could be one for the pot. Brown crabs are pretty easy to handle and can be quite docile but the velvet swimmers get a little feisty. Also known as devil crabs, you can tell which ones they are by their mad red eyes. Take care or they will give you a nip.

Velvet swimmers aren't eaten much in the UK but they are a delicacy in Spain and Portugal. To land them for the pot they must be over 65 mm across the carapace. That might seem a little small but it's worth the fiddle to get the flesh out. They are delicious.

Before boiling, carefully lift up the flap between their legs and push a sharp pointed object, such as a small screwdriver, into the small indentation underneath. This will disable the crab instantly. Next, poke the screwdriver between the eyes and into the shell to kill them.

Boil for about 10 minutes in seawater then break them open by prising the two halves of the shell apart. Remove the innards and the 'dead men's fingers' or gills of the crab and discard. Pick out the shell and crack the claws with the end of a spoon to remove all the meat.

simple velvet
SWIMMER CRAB WITH PASTA

◀ Mix the crab meat with a little white wine vinegar and season well. Cook some fresh pasta and mix the crab meat with the pasta. Add a dash of cream and drizzle with a squeeze of lemon juice and a smattering of chopped parsley. Enjoy!

FRASER'S PATENTED PRAWN CATCHER

The great thing about my friend Fraser's patented prawn catcher is that he hasn't patented it at all, which is why he's more than happy for me to share it with you here. It's a very simple but very clever device that can be used to catch shrimps and prawns. In fact, it is so simple that it's stupidly simple (!) and I don't know why someone hasn't thought of it before. I suppose they have. It's called a lobster pot. Anyway, this is it.

Actually it isn't, because I need to tell you something first that is very important. Fraser's shrimp catcher requires the use of plastic bottles. So you must not, under any circumstances, forget where you put them or put them in a place where they are likely to get washed away by the tide or lost to the sea. Whilst the prawn catcher recycles old bottles and puts them to use once more (which is good) there is a risk that they can get away and end up with all the other bits of rubbish choking the marine environment (which is very bad indeed).

What you need is a knife, an old plastic bottle (2 litre fizzy drink type is best) and some bait.

- ★ With your knife, cut the top off the bottle just below where the neck starts to narrow.
- ★ Stand the bottle upright and then turn the top of the bottle upside down so it drops back into the bottle.
- ★ Now cut a couple of nicks of about ½ cm in one side of the top, on the edge that you have just cut, about a centimetre apart. Repeat on the opposite side.
- ★ Cut a 1 cm long slit on the bottle about 1 cm below the rim.
- ★ Push the top of the bottle into the rest of it and place the tabs in the top into the slit in the bottom so that it is secured in place.
- ★ Bait the pot with bits of fish guts or flesh and place in pools or under rock ledges at low tide. Make sure it is secured and can't get away and that you know where it is.
- ★ As with a lobster pot, prawns will be able to get in but not out again.
- ★ Return at the next low tide and see what's in the pot.

Once you've got your prawns it's up to you what to do with them. Some people like to put them back or just keep the biggest ones. If you go for the latter, boil up some seawater over a beach fire and eat them there and then. If you've remembered the mayo, dip them before you eat them. Or how about a prawn cocktail? Mix up salad cream and tomato ketchup for your very own Marie Rose sauce. Classy!

This is one for the first pickings of the autumn and the last barbecue of the summer. Time to get your hands dirty. It'll be worth it. But first, here are some mussel-picking rules

★ Pick mussels on low spring tides when you'll be able to get to the biggest ones.

★ Don't take all the biggest mussels from a clump. Pick selectively.

★ Don't pick mussels from just anywhere; dirty rivers and outfalls pollute shellfish. Plump, clean mussels can generally be found at low tide at the ends of piers and jetties – but please take care and don't fall in.

★ Pick mussels with no (or few) barnacles or seaweed as they will be easier to clean. To clean them, scrub them with a brush, ideally under cold running water, and remove any 'beards'. Discard any mussels that don't close when given a sharp tap.

★ De-grit the mussels by leaving them in a bucket of fresh water with a dash of vinegar for at least half an hour before cooking.

★ Don't try to eat any mussels that refuse to open during cooking.

Now you can start cooking. These three ways are really easy and will give you a gorgeous taste of the sea within minutes.

moules with GARLIC BUTTER

◀ Firstly, pick out all the biggest mussels, say about 20. Boil up about an inch of seawater in a big pan with a lid and chuck the mussels in. Let them steam for about 5 minutes or until they open. Once they have opened, take the pan off the heat and drain the mussels, then remove and discard the empty half shell of each one. Put a dab of butter in each meaty shell, along with a smidge of crushed garlic and a little finely chopped parsley. Very carefully, place each mussel on the barbecue and cook them for another minute or so until the butter begins to bubble. Eat them from the shells.

moules in a FOIL PARCEL

◀ If you have no other receptacle to cook in, foil will work brilliantly. Prepare and clean the mussels and place a couple of handfuls on a large square of kitchen foil. Gather up the edges and add a dash of white wine, cider or beer, some chopped parsley and a finely chopped shallot. Now seal the edges of the foil to make a parcel and place it on the barbecue. Let the mussels steam away for a few minutes and then open up the parcel and eat.

◀ Fancy something a little different? Try hot smoking your moules. It couldn't be easier and will give them a beautiful dark and smoky flavour (see page 183)

Coastal adventures

TAKE A HIKE! WALK THE COAST PATH

You don't need me to tell you that walking is good. It just is. It's what our bodies were made for. And it's undeniably nice to walk along the coast path and see inlets and islands, sands and shingles, bluffs and beaches, cliffs and coves. There's an awful lot of it to see. Perfect then, for an autumn day.

The UK has approximately 11,000 miles of coastline, with England claiming 2,748 miles of it. But of course, walking along it isn't as simple as you might think. Despite our love affair with the coast, almost a thousand miles of coastline has no 'satisfactory, legally secure access', according to Natural England. Scotland and Wales, similarly, have no continuous path around their coast – though plans are afoot (get it?) to put this right. In fact, the Welsh coastal path is due to open in summer 2012. This is good news for walkers who intend to circumnavigate the UK coastline one step at a time, but not much use for those of us with other transport to worry about.

And this leads us to a seemingly unimportant but actually quite important question: what happens to the van? Do you walk along and then walk back? Do you find a circular route? Do you send Mother on ahead to pick you up? Take two vehicles? It's all a bit of a conundrum (and yes, it is worth discussing). Personally I can't stand turning back on myself on a walk because I like to see new things all the time. A circular route is always preferable, but a linear route is best when tackling the coast path. Surely?

Thankfully, solutions have been devised. In Pembrokeshire, for example, they have a coastal bus service that covers the path, meaning you can walk a bit then get the bus back to your van or the campsite where you started. It's not exactly rocket science but it does answer the basic problem. And, get this: the routes have amazing names. So, if you fancy a day out walking the coast path between Fishguard and Cardigan, you could well find yourself aboard the Poppit Rocket. You could also step on board the Coastal Cruiser, the Strumble Shuttle or the Celtic Coaster. Brilliant, brilliant stuff. I love it already.

THE UK'S BEST COASTAL PATHS

PEMBROKESHIRE COASTAL PATH: Once again this beautiful part of the UK gets top prize. The Pembrokeshire Coastal Bus Service (www.pembrokeshire.gov.uk/coastbus) covers all 186 miles of it and passes some of the UK's loveliest beaches. In fact you'll pass 58 beaches and 14 harbours if you walk its entire length. One day Bob the Dog and I intend to finish what we started when we wrote 'Dog Walks of Pembrokeshire with Bob the Dog' in which we included a few of the best coastal walks. But until then you're on your own.

THE NORFOLK COAST PATH: This National Trail traverses the coast from Hunstanton to Cromer. It scores second place because the name of its bus service, the Coasthopper (www.coasthopper.co.uk), isn't quite in the same league as the Poppit Rocket. Never mind. This is a top place to see wide open beaches, collect crabs and take a stomp in the English countryside. Good for disabled access with entire sections that are negotiable by wheelchair or for pushchairs.

THE SOUTH WEST COAST PATH: At 630 miles long, this is the daddy of all the trails. No coastal bus service but lots of transport options, including trains and buses. A word of warning though: get the transport there and walk back. That way you won't have to worry about missing a connection. They can be a bit few and far between. www.southwestcoastpath.com has all the info you'll need.

THE CLEVELAND WAY: I used to surf along this part of the coast way back when. The coastal section of this second of the National Trails, from Scarborough to Saltburn by the Sea, takes in some really lovely towns and villages, beaches and harbours including Staithes, Sandsend, Robin Hood's Bay and Runswick Bay. There are railway stations at Whitby, Saltburn and Scarborough and bus stops along the way; www.yorkshiretravel.net has a journey planner, which will help you to plan your walks.

THE CUMBRIAN WAY: This coastal romp takes in some of the UK's prettiest coast including St Bees Head, home to large colonies of seabirds. For day trips the stretch between Barrow in Furness and Maryport is perfect because the Cumbrian Coast Line runs along the entire route. Park up, get a ticket, enjoy the ride along the coast, walk back. Train times and routes from www.nationalrail.co.uk.

THE LLYN COASTAL PATH: Just one more reason to visit North Wales. You might even feel a little righteous doing it. In many places the coastal path follows the ancient pilgrimage route to Bardsey Island, once a Christian Shrine. From Caernarfon it's 91 miles along the coast to Porthmadog. The Cambrian Line runs between Pwhelli and Porthmadog whilst buses ziz-zag their way across the peninsula. Check travel details at www.gwynedd.gov.uk and ww.thecambrianline.co.uk.

THE AYRSHIRE COASTAL PATH: Almost three-quarters of this 84-mile Scottish trail will have you walking along the beach. The rest is over cliffs, through towns and along promenades. Buses are frequent and there's a good webby wotsit (www.ayrshirecoastalpath.org) showing you where you can walk. Great views to Arran and Ireland and plenty of ancient harbours and smugglers' caves along the way.

THE MORAY COASTAL TRAIL: Fifty miles of waymarked trail (www.morayways. org.uk) show you the way from Forres to Cullen on the Moray coast in Scotland. Along the way you'll see all sorts – dolphins, seabirds, spectacular cliffs and light-houses. The Inverness to Aberdeen train only stops at Forres and Elgin but there are buses. www.travelinescotland.com.

Bellyboarding: or, you're never too old to take to the sea

If you've never surfed, then bellyboarding is the place to start. And I'm not talking about Morey Boogie boards with slick bottoms and carbon fibre inserts or polystyrene bellyboards or even those cheap and nasty plastic boards that you can buy from just about any beach shop in Britain. What I am talking about is the original wooden surfboard, as used by our grannies and grandads – and maybe even our great grannies and great grandads – on their holidays to Cornwall in the fifties and sixties.

> **SEASIDE SECRETS:** Some of the earliest bellyboards were simply made from planks of wood about 5' x 1' x 1/2" thick, known as coffin lid boards. In fact, one of the chief manufacturers was an undertaker, Tremewan, in Perranporth, Cornwall, who saw an opening in the market. It wasn't until the 1930s that marine-ply boards, with the upturned nose, began to appear. To see some early examples, visit the British Surfing Museum in Devon, www.museumofbritishsurfing.org.uk

GETTING STARTED

Bellyboarding is an incredibly easy way to enjoy the thrill of the glide but without having to go through the rigmarole of learning to paddle out or stand up. And that's why it spans the generations. Take a dip with a plank under your arm and you'll be joining a great British seaside tradition that, thankfully, refuses to die out.

First you'll need a board. You might be lucky and find one lurking at the back of a beach store near you (or even at the back of the garage), but in case you have no luck, get in contact with Sally at the Original Surfboard Company. She makes handcrafted boards in the original way and sells them through www.originalsurfboards.co.uk. They are lovely objects and can be custom-painted to suit you and your van. An added benefit is that they take up hardly any space in the van, are more environmentally friendly than mass-produced boards and will give any coastal outing a wonderful, nostalgic feel. Just don't forget to pack your flowery swimming cap and your mum's old swimsuit.

Any sandy beach where there are waves is perfect. You don't even have to wait for the right type of waves. A rough sea might be tricky, but it's still possible.

the *Original Surfboard* company

Made in Britain

The how-to bit

★ Wade out into the waves until you are waist deep.

★ Turn your back to the waves and hold your bellyboard out in front of you with both hands at the top.

★ The bottom of the board should rest approximately at your waist or thighs.

★ When a wave comes along, wait until it is about a yard or so from you, then project yourself towards the beach, lying prone on your board as you go.

★ The wave, with any luck, will pick you up and transport you towards the shore in a rush of watery excitement! Now you're surfing.

TIP: Catching unbroken waves (before they become white water) will give you more speed and a better rush. If you're happy in the sea, grab a pair of flippers and try it that way. You'll catch even bigger waves further out.

THE WORLD BELLYBOARDING CHAMPIONSHIPS

It happens on the first Sunday in September in Chapel Porth, Cornwall.

If you fancy taking part in one of surfing's most unusual events, then this is for you. It might even be worth turning up just for a look and a great day out. Expect over 200 keen entrants (some in period costumes) and a wonderful, back to basics competition, organised and run by the National Trust (www.bellyboarding.co.uk). We absolutely adore it.

Darkening days

The autumnal equinox occurs around 22nd–23rd of September. This is the day on which the sun spends an equal amount of time above and below the horizon, and is directly over the equator on its annual cycle. It's pretty much when day equals night and brings some of the biggest tides of the year. Before long, it will be the last Sunday in October: the day when the clocks go back one hour to Greenwich Mean Time from British Summer Time. With the sun dipping down below the horizon at around 5 pm, this creates an indeterminate time between dark and bed. Which means you might just have to make your own fun.

SURVIVING LONG NIGHTS

SEEING IS BELIEVING Going for a walk at dusk is a brilliant way to adjust your eyes to the lack of daylight. It can extend the day by an hour or so.

PACK A WIND-UP Wind-up torches are very eco-marvellous but they are also very useful because they don't run out of batteries just when you need them most.

GAMES THAT NEVER END The top locker is for the fun stuff. I've said it before. At this time of year it's a good idea to remove the bunting and the swimming goggles and replace it with a selection of games. Compendiums are good, cards essential, bulky games like Buckaroo downright inconvenient. Try Mille Bornes, the classic French driving game that can go on for hours. How appropriate. Or how about making up your own Camper Van Top Trumps? I shouldn't have said that should I? Someone will do it now. Anyway, think of your favourite 20 camper van conversions and set them off against each other. Maybe not.

BRING OUT THE PC Got a long battery life or hooked up to the electric? Watch a DVD or do some work. Eh? You never heard me say that.

GO DIGITAL For long journeys and dark nights the Nintendo DS is a little electronic marvel. Dad's little digital helper. But only in small doses or they forget how to communicate.

RUB-A-DUB-DUB As if you hadn't thought of that? You know the drill: eke out a pint for as long as possible, get the best seat next to the fire, refuse to move.

CHEESE fondue

Fancy cooking something that belongs to a time closer to your van's age? This is it.
If you want to make a meal of it (so to speak), cook some new potatoes too and use
those, as well as the bread, to dip into the cheese.

FOR 4

400G GRUYÈRE CHEESE

200G EMMENTHAL CHEESE

2 TSP CORNFLOUR

2 TBSP KIRSCH

1 CLOVE GARLIC

200MLS OF DRY WHITE WINE

WHOLE NUTMEG, FOR GRATING

202
AUTUMN

TO SERVE

CHUNKS OF BREAD, CORNICHONS AND CRUDITÉS (SUCH AS CARROTS, FENNEL, RADISHES)

A GREEN SALAD DRESSED WITH A LEMONY VINAIGRETTE

Grate the cheeses. In a cup, mix the cornflour with the Kirsch.

Peel the garlic and halve it, then drop it into a medium-sized pan. Pour in the wine
and bring to simmering point.

Add the grated cheeses to the bubbling wine, in handfuls, stirring or whisking in
between each addition. Finally, stir in the kirsch mixture, a generous grating of nutmeg
and some freshly ground pepper. You will now have a lovely thick unctuous molten
cheese deliciousness.

Put the pan in the middle of the table and let everyone dig in with chunks of bread
speared on forks, or with cornichons and crudités. Accompany with the green salad. If
the fondue thickens and cools, reheat it gently.

rainy day POPCORN

Got bored kids? Watch their little faces light up with an afternoon popping popcorn.
Pans with glass lids add to the excitement.

Parmesan and lemon

FOR 2

1 TBSP VEGETABLE OIL
3 TBSP POPCORN MAIZE
3 TBSP BUTTER
3-4 TBSP FINELY GRATED PARMESAN
ZEST OF A LEMON
PINCH OR TWO OF CRUSHED DRIED CHILLIES, OPTIONAL

Heat the oil in a large pan. Tip in the maize and cover the pan. Pop the corn over a
medium giving the pan a shake now and then – you will know when it is ready as the
popping will stop. At the same time, melt the butter in a small pan.

Tip the popcorn into a large bowl. Add the melted butter, parmesan, lemon zest, a
generous pinch of crushed sea salt and the chillies, if using. Toss together and eat while warm.

Maple and cinnamon

FOR 2

1 TBSP VEGETABLE OIL
3 TBSP POPCORN MAIZE
3 TBSP BUTTER
3 TBSP MAPLE SYRUP
1 TSP GROUND CINNAMON
SEA SALT FLAKES

Heat the oil in a large pan. Tip in the maize and cover the pan. Pop the corn over a
medium heat for 5 minutes or so – give the pan a shake now and then as it cooks.

Meanwhile, melt the butter in a small pan with the maple syrup and cinnamon.

When the popping has subsided, tip the corn into a large bowl, pour in the butter
mixture, add a couple of pinches of crushed sea salt and toss together.

FRYING PAN mini pizzas

Pizza in the van? Who'd have thought it? But you can, as Sarah's recipe proves. No need for complicated directions for the takeaway driver. Do it yourself! Don't take too long or you'll have to give yourself a pound off.

MAKES 8 SMALL PIZZAS
1½ MUGFULS STRONG WHITE
   FLOUR (300G), PLUS EXTRA FOR KNEADING
7G SACHET EASY-BAKE DRIED YEAST
1 TSP SUGAR
2 TBSP OLIVE OIL, PLUS EXTRA FOR FRYING

FOR THE TOPPING
8 RIPE TOMATOES
½ TSP SUGAR
OLIVE OIL
3 BALLS MOZZARELLA, DRAINED
   AND TORN INTO SMALL PIECES
HANDFUL BASIL LEAVES, TORN

Put the flour, yeast, teaspoon of sugar, 2 tablespoons of olive oil and half a teaspoon of salt into a large bowl. Add 200mls warm water. Mix with a large spoon and then, using your hands, bring the dough together and into a ball.

Transfer the sticky dough to a floured surface and knead for 5 minutes. Put the dough into a clean bowl, cover with a damp tea towel and leave for 45 minutes-1 hour to rise and double in size. Meanwhile, chop the tomatoes and simmer in a pan with the sugar and a slug of olive oil for 7-10 minutes, until you have a chunky sauce. Season.

Preheat the grill and heat a tablespoon of oil in a frying pan. Tip the dough onto the work surface and divide it into eight pieces. Using your fingers, gently stretch a piece into a saucer-sized circle. Fry in the sizzling oil for 3-4 minutes on each side until puffed and golden. Transfer to your grill pan and top with tomato sauce and mozzarella. Grill for 2-3 minutes till bubbling. Scatter with basil and eat. Repeat with the other pieces of dough. If you can fit them under the grill, you can do more than one at a time – top them while they are hot and grill as soon as possible.

TIP: This dough also makes great dough balls – divide into 30 small pieces and roll into balls. Fry the balls for 5-6 minutes, turning them, and toss in garlic butter.

olive, rosemary and
REAL ALE DAMPER BREAD

If you ever thought you couldn't cook bread out on the trail, think again. It doesn't even have to be wrapped around a dirty stick. Damper bread can be made in all kinds of ways but is always based on the principle of simplicity and easy-to-carry ingredients. Perfect for a camper then.

Basically flour, butter and water, damper bread was traditionally cooked in the Outback in the embers of a fire. You can cook it this way too but I would recommend using a Dutch oven – a heavy cast iron cooking pot with small legs and a lipped concave lid that is designed to have hot embers shovelled on to the top without ruining the food inside – as this will give an all-over heat. The lid can also be turned upside down for cooking eggs. How about that for versatility? Those clever Aussies.

Anyway, the tricky bit with this is regulating the temperature so that you get an even heat throughout the Dutch oven and don't burn the bread underneath. Trust me, I know. That's why the lipped lid is so vital. Eat the bread with hot soup and lashings of bad-but-so-right butter.

◀ MAKES 1 LOAF
3½ MUGS (750G) SELF-RAISING FLOUR
50G SOFT BUTTER, CHOPPED, PLUS EXTRA FOR GREASING
3 CLOVES GARLIC, FINELY CHOPPED
HALF A CUP (100G) CHOPPED PITTED BLACK OLIVES
HANDFUL CHOPPED FRESH ROSEMARY
½ TSP SUGAR
½ TSP SALT
350MLS REAL ALE, SUCH AS SHARP'S DOOM BAR BITTER (OR YOU CAN USE MILK OR
    WATER OR HALF AND HALF OF EACH, IF YOU PREFER)

First build and light a fire.

To make the bread, tip the flour into a mixing bowl, rub in the butter. Add the garlic, olives, rosemary, sugar and salt and mix together. Now, dribble in the ale, a little at a time, mixing as you do so. Next, using your hands, bring the dough together and into a ball. Flatten the ball slightly then cut a cross in the top with a sharp knife and place in a lightly buttered Dutch oven. Dust the top of the bread with flour.

Put the Dutch oven in the embers of a fire (oh I get it, that's why it has little legs). Make sure you have enough embers to shovel on to the lid. Don't allow the fire to flame or get too hot, otherwise the bread will burn. Leave in the embers for approximately 30-40 minutes to cook. Check it after 20 minutes to see how it is getting on. When it is ready, it will sound hollow when tapped.

If you want to make this at home, it also works well baked at 200°C/fan 100°C/ Gas 6 for the same amount of time.

Take in the sea air

A STROLL ALONG THE PIERS OF BRITAIN

If you're looking for a symbol of the British seaside, it has to be the pleasure pier. They are icons of our seaside's magnificent past, when ladies changed in huts and men wore woollen swimmers and waxed moustaches. In those pre-jet-setting times, when the seaside was the place to take a break, a resort could be judged by the size and splendour of its piers. They were places where wheezing city folk could take in the sea air, get themselves thoroughly entertained and have a bite to eat. Nowt wrong with that.

From Southend's magnificent mile-and-a-bit long protrusion to Cleveden's Grade One listed, wrought-iron masterpiece, there are almost 60 surviving pleasure piers. In my book, they are a special treat that we save for high days and holidays when we're careering around the coast and fancy a little bit of that kiss-me-quick brashness. We love the penny arcades and the sense of escape that they give us. We let go of our seek-out-deserted-sands mentality and dive in head first for some pure and simple, unsophisticated fun. A whizz on a waltzer, a cone of chips and back to the van in time for tea. Campervantastic!

Here is our list of the very best of Britain's piers. It's been compiled on few criteria other than it must be unusual – the longest, oddest, oldest, whatever. Go with it, but don't forget the rest of them (at www.piers.org.uk). Without our ice cream-loving souls to save them, they may yet be lost to the sea forever.

CLEVEDON PIER, Somerset www.clevedonpier.com
My favourite. Built in 1869, it is still splendid and the only intact Grade One listed pier in the UK. With no amusements or rides or brashness, this is a genteel pier for a Sunday stroll and a slice of lemon drizzle cake in the café at the end.

BRIGHTON PIER, East Sussex www.brightonpier.co.uk
Fast and huge rides, modern amusements, with many of the original features intact.

SOUTHWOLD PIER, Suffolk www.southwoldpier.co.uk
Very tasteful, very nicely done pier with the best amusements ever at the Under the Pier Show in a great seaside town. Classy!

SOUTHEND ON SEA, Essex www.sarfend.co.uk/southendpier.html
Damaged by fire on several occasions, but still the world's longest pleasure pier with a train that runs its length.

BOSCOMBE PIER, Dorset www.inspieration.org
Stylish postmodern structure and Grade Two listed entrance. Pier of the Year 2010.

YARMOUTH BRITANNIA PIER, Norfolk www.britannia-pier.co.uk
Amusements, rides and one of the last pier theatres. Catch Jim Davidson, Cannon and Ball, Basil Brush and more.

SWANAGE PIER, Dorset www.swanagepiertrust.com
Beneath the waves is one of the UK's best-sheltered diving spots. If you prefer to stay dry, there's an underwater camera at the end of this beautifully restored Victorian pier.

EASTBOURNE PIER, East Sussex www.the-pier.co.uk/eastbourne-pier
Refined, elegant, quintessentially English and the only pier in the world to have its own camera obscura.

BLACKPOOL CENTRAL PIER, Lancashire www.attractionsblackpool.co.uk
This is the house of fun. The 108-foot Ferris wheel might make you feel a bit Tom and Dick but the views from the top are amazing. The Legends Show is the place to catch all the very best tributes. Blobby Williams? Not half!

LLANDUDNO PIER, Conwy www.llandudnoonline.co.uk/pages/pier.html
The longest pier in Wales, designed so punters can see out to sea as well as back to the land. Popular location for period dramas.

SEASIDE SECRETS: How do they make seaside rock?

It's actually very simple, once you've seen it done. Rock is made from water, sugar and glucose that's boiled and then cooled and has colouring added to it. The letters are made by taking long strips of coloured candy and putting them together with strips of white. This is then wrapped around a big candy core. Then it's stretched and rolled out by vicious-looking finger-nipping rollers. That's basically it. Kind of. But if you need more, go and see it being made for yourself at Docwra's Rock Shop in Great Yarmouth (the world's biggest, apparently). Oh yes, and they do make spelling mistakes from time to time.

Take a roller coaster ride

The Big Dipper is the roller coaster that gave its name to all roller coasters. It's the UK's oldest working roller coaster and has been at Blackpool Pleasure Beach since 1923. It's dwarfed by The Big One these days but still provides a few thrills. We rode it. The general consensus was 'Oh-m-geee, that was brilliant!' Mind you, that was a couple of weeks later. At the time, all Charlie could say was, 'I want to get off. I want to get off.' It was too late by then.

There are some people who would travel to the ends of the earth to try out a new ride and there are those who can take or leave them. I am of the latter variety. Even so, riding a roller coaster is something that you simply must do if you go to the seaside. Those are the rules. Here are some of the best of the best.

BLACKPOOL PLEASURE BEACH is the king of seaside parks worldwide. Full stop. Home to Charlie's nemesis, The Big Dipper, a ride that's as old-fashioned as they come – it looks like a coaster should and feels rickety too. You can also ride The Big One (at 235 feet tall it's one of Europe's highest) and The Grand National (Europe's first, dual-track coaster).

GREAT YARMOUTH PLEASURE BEACH has a traditional wooden roller coaster that was built in France in 1928 and then transported to Great Yarmouth five years later. Free entry means you can just stroll in and wander around. So if you were in the area you could go ride the roller coaster for three quid. Nice. And no messing about with wristbands.

ADVENTURE ISLAND IN SOUTHEND is another free entry park and, as Justin Garanovich, ace roller coaster fan and founder of the European Coaster Club put it, it's a 'great example of how a small seaside park can be made to work'. That said, there's nothing cute or cuddly about Rage, their newest roller coaster. Its loops and twists and near-vertical drops are 'for superheroes only'. Charlie would not approve. Right next to Southend's very long pier. Kill two birds.

KLONDIKE is the resident roller coaster at Funland in Hayling Island. A fun, small, family-owned park with a good collection of rides as well as the signature upside-down roller coaster.

THE TURBO COASTER ON BRIGHTON PIER is my choice because it's on the end of a pier and does a loop-the-loop and was the first coaster I ever rode. There are moments when it's just you and the sea and the sky and the feeling that you could fall off at any moment. Happy seaside memories! They also have a Crazy Mouse mini coaster, which Charlie tried out in Paignton. She didn't think much of that one either.

DREAMLAND, MARGATE The final coaster on the list is one to watch out for. One of the oldest surviving roller coasters in the world, it is now a Grade Two listed building. It was built in 1920 and is due to re-open as part of a new heritage park in 2013 (after restoration by the Dreamland Trust). Watch this space, so to speak.

The best coastal driving routes

Once the summer hordes have gone you'll (more or less) have the road to yourself. What better way to enjoy a little you time than to take the old girl for a spin before she takes a break for winter? I'm not talking about a quick dash around the block. I'm talking about having a last blast drive along a proper coast road.

I've been very careful with my definition here, so you can expect genuine roads along the coast rather than roads with occasional coastal glimpses. In my opinion these are the very best driving roads in Britain, with vistas, cliffs, tiny coves and harbours where you can blow away the cobwebs and have a blast.

THE CAUSEWAY COAST, Northern Ireland

Now that's what I'm talking about. This has been described as one of the best driving roads in the world and I know why. From Larne to Portrush you'll be treated to some of the most spectacular coastal scenery anywhere. For a large part of the drive, the road actually hugs the coast on the very thin strip between mountains and sea so you follow the contours of the coast all the way. Great stop-offs include the Giant's Causeway itself and the Carrick-a-Rede rope bridge, both touristy attractions. A diversion to Farr Head will have the clutch squealing but it's worth it, despite the hairpins and steep ascents. Your van will love it.

FROM ABERAERON TO PORTHMADOG, West Wales

This road is a cracker. With sweeping curves that take you to the finest viewing points along the coast, it's one of those roads that just keeps on getting better the further you go. At the points where you head inland you'll still get to enjoy estuaries, funny old bridges and gorgeous valleys. It won't disappoint, not ever. From Tywyn, looking north towards Barmouth, the views are really lovely, especially on a sunny day. Aberdovey is worth a stop too.

THE COPPER COAST, Southern Ireland

I have driven the short stretch of road that makes up the copper coast between Dungarvan and Tramore many times in the vain hope that I might find some surf. Even so, it never disappoints, particularly when it comes to coastal vistas. There are some excellent beaches along the way, including Stradbally and Bunmahon and some very impressive old mine workings near Annestown that look spooky in the mist. You'll also pass the church at Fenor, which is where I got married. Awwww. Bless.

THE RING OF KERRY, Ireland

There's an etiquette that says you have to drive anti-clockwise around the Ring of Kerry. But if you are a camper van driver and don't mind heading towards enormous coaches coming at you down narrow, badly surfaced roads you can always go the other way. It's up to you. Anyway, the stretch between Kenmare and Waterville is the best and the views overlooking Derrynane Beach as you head south from Waterville are divine. Good place for a stop and a brew. If you need an Aran jumper, Sneem is the place to get it. Pack a sou'wester and go.

PORTREATH TO SENNEN COVE, Cornwall

This can be a bit convoluted but it's worth the bother. Between Portreath and St Ives you'll pass a few sandy surfing beaches and tourist towns as well as a fabulous view over North Beach. Then it's to St Ives, a busy town that's not great for a drive-by but brilliant for a detour to see the Tate Gallery and Porthmeor beach. If you're running low on fudge or art, it's good for shopping too. Beyond St Ives, it gets a bit wild. That's when it gets really good. The winding road to Zennor passes perfect farms and old mine workings and offers detours to Cape Cornwall and walks up granite tors. At Sennen you can breathe a bit, with a coffee, overlooking one of Cornwall's best beaches. Oh yes. I love it.

CROMER TO HUNSTANTON, Norfolk

This is altogether different but not unpleasant. It's not a coast hugger – and by that I mean that it doesn't flit along the coast the entire way – but it's very pretty all the same, with lots of opportunities for detours to wide open beaches, windmills, ruined priories and cutesy antique shops. Plus, you get the added benefit of being able to get fresh Cromer crab and take in a Seaside Special show on Cromer pier, which is, of course, not to be beaten. Crab sandwich anyone? Legend has it there are also waves at Runton. So they say.

FRESHWATER TO SANDOWN, Isle of Wight

While you're there you might as well just circumnavigate the island. It won't take long and you'll pass through salt-smelling beach towns, along crumbling cliffs, over tall headlands and past idyllic estuaries. Not all the road is coastal but the part of it that is – the section from Freshwater to Niton – is nothing short of spectacular. Heading west you see the white chalk cliffs that make up the needles, as well as the lovely Compton Bay, as the road skirts along the edge of the cliffs. Lots of stopping places and lots of charm. I love it.

NEWHAVEN TO WORTHING, Sussex

Some of the coastal drives I have done are jaw-dropping. This one isn't. But it is the very best of the best when it comes to cruising the prom. Heck, you don't even have to do the whole thing. There are enough miles of wide esplanades, Georgian-fronted hotels and genteel squares to keep you amused between Brighton and Hove. And of course plenty of stop-offs for ice cream, amusements and seaside fun along the way. There aren't many spots to park up for the night, but that's not what it's for is it? Among the coastal drives, this is the one for the show and shine.

THE WEST COAST OF SCOTLAND

Yes, I know it's not a route and I know there are loads of options and yes I know you sometimes have to go inland. But flipping heck! Any drive to the Highlands is going to take you past sea lochs and along winding coastal roads that are just so pretty your eyes will hurt.* You'll drive over box girder bridges, raging torrents and through small hamlets with amazing-looking pubs. Why not pop over to Skye and drive around there too? Amazing. Just go.

*Not really.

Visit a wind farm

If the wind puffs a bit it could be a good day to go see it do something wonderful. Autumn, with the first breaths of winter winding up to blow the awning off your van, is perfect for visiting wind farms.

I know that I am going to sound like a right old hippy, but I adore wind farms. They represent a faith in the future. I don't really care if they aren't that efficient, if they're noisy, spoil someone's view or make your house prices plummet. I believe they are graceful, majestic things and that we should revere them for what they do. We should thank our lucky stars that they never found coal in some of our most beautiful coastal areas, or that we didn't have to give up our view for a slag heap. And let's not forget that they can be taken down again when we've worked out a more efficient way of generating energy without harming the environment.

The Whitelee Wind Farm in Scotland creates enough power to provide electricity for 180,000 homes every year. That's not to be sniffed at. Especially when you remember that this is clean energy. And 180,000 homes is in the region of a city the size of York. Oh yes, and by the way, the RSPB only objects to about 7% of wind farm planning proposals on the basis that the turbines will risk killing birds because of their location. So, take that NIMBYs. Find a different argument.

There are thousands of wind farms all over the UK that are there for you to gawp at in wonder. I have listed just a few that can be seen easily from the coast. Go and see what they do. And spend five minutes enjoying them for what they give us – hope.

Those with visitor centres:

SCROBY SANDS, GREAT YARMOUTH is one of the UK's first commercial offshore wind farms.
SHERINGHAM SHOAL WINDFARM (www.scira.co.uk) is currently under construction, but should be fully operational by the time you get down there.
THANET is the largest offshore wind farm in the world, with 100 turbines.
WHITELEE WINDFARM (www.whiteleewindfarm.co.uk) is Europe's largest wind farm.

A few others…

BURBO BANK AND BRISTOW WIND FARMS What a stunning backdrop these turbines give to Gormley's Another Place on Crosby Beach. Kill two birds with one stone. See some art, admire the current generating view.
FULLABROOK WIND FARM NORTH DEVON. Twenty-two new turbines dominate the skyline of North Devon. And very nice they are too. Some locals don't like 'em but I say whoopee. I can almost see them from my house.
MORWENSTOW WIND FARM Just a wee gem of a wind farm this one. Three turbines laugh in the face of the naysayers on the North Cornwall coast.
RHYL FLATS WIND FARM Off the North Wales coast. Thirty turbines capable of producing 90 MW of power.

For more on renewable energy and wind farms, visit www.bwea.com.

The best bridges. The best way home

I'm all for going the long way around, but sometimes you just want to get there and get the kettle on. It's a philosophy that's inspired many an engineer, road builder and dreamer as they have endeavoured to find a decent short cut between here and there. The result? Bridges.

I say, if you can, take the bridge. They are sensational things, engineering's superstars, spanning physical and spiritual divides. They make our lives easier, our trade routes shorter and our lives more connected. They keep our feet dry. And, when they are built with flair and imagination, they become wonderful additions to our landscape. Great bridges are icons.

My good friend Martin Knight is an architect who specialises in building bridges. Martin is also a camper van owner. He likes nothing more than pootling around in his van in his stovepipe hat visiting the country's finest bridges. Here are his favourites.

OLDEST: The Union Bridge
Europe's oldest surviving suspension bridge was built by a Royal Navy officer, Captain Samuel Brown, between 1819 and 1820. The roadway, which is timber and suspended from pairs of wrought-iron chains, still carries traffic between England and Scotland. It's a little out of the way now, but worth a detour.

BEST THREE-IN-ONE: The Severn River Crossings
There are two Severn crossings, but actually three bridges. You can drive them all in a loop but you won't save any money on tolls that way. At some point you're going to have to pay to get into Wales. It's free to leave. Anyway, the original Severn crossing is made up of two bridges. One of them spans the Wye and it's the prettiest. The new crossing is the longest in the UK at 5 kilometres from end to end.

MOST BRIDGE-LIKE: Humber Bridge
A big old structure that's 155 metres tall and 2,200 metres long, at its central span – that's the longest in the UK. It joins North Lincolnshire with the East Riding of Yorkshire and so connects two very different communities. What building bridges is all about.

CURLIEST: Kylescu Bridge, Scottish Highlands

Look at this bridge and you can't help but go awwwwwww. It's the way it bends as it crosses the sea passage of Loch a' Chàirn Bhàin that makes it so appealing – and also makes it one of the most beautiful on this list.

PRETTIEST: The Tyne Bridges

The Tyne is famous for its bridges. Unfortunately you can't drive over the very lovely Millennium Gateshead Bridge (which Martin designed) but you get a cracking view of it from the Tyne Bridge, which is OK too. Actually, it's one of those structures that deserves more than a passing mention. An icon if ever there was one. Wor!

MOST MONSTROUS: Forth Road Bridge, East Scotland

This absolute monster is over 2.5 kilometres long and 156 metres high. Do they really never finish painting it? Enjoy amazing views of the Forth Bridge, its rail-carrying neighbour, as you cross.

HUMPIEST: Skye Bridge

At one time you'd have had to take a ferry to the Isle of Skye, but now you can drive. That's going to have a big impact isn't it? For the best? Who knows? From some angles it looks like a humpbacked bridge on a very big scale.

ODDEST: Middlesbrough Transporter Bridge

Transporter bridges are odd things in that their span provides a support for an under-slung gondola that crosses the river on wires. Eh? I know. This is the only working example in England so it's very special. You drive on, stop the van and wait. The whole bridge then moves you to the other side. It's like a giant zip wire! Only nine cars at a time. Bless.

LEAST ORGANISED: Bideford Old Bridge, Devon

I go over and under this bridge on a regular basis. Each of its 24 stone-built arches is a different size. It's quirky and looks lovely at dusk. There has been a bridge on this site since 1286 so I guess it just sort of evolved that way.

MOST LIKE A CASTLE: Conwy Suspension Bridge, North Wales

This is one of the world's first crenellated suspension bridges and it's under the very impressive turrets of Conwy Castle, itself an architectural wonder. Designed by the prolific Thomas Telford and opened in 1826.

COMFORT FOOD: Recipes for autumn

In many ways we need our comfort food more in the autumn than in the winter. That's to stop the first sniffles from taking hold. After a summer of outdoor living, a storm or two can be a shock to the system. Coax it back to life with some autumn comforts. At the very least, go scrumping.

the breakfast BURRITO

This recipe is testament to all that is great about the camper van community. I got it from a guy called Ian Telford. He sent it to me because he wanted to share a little of his experience of surfing, cooking and eating. So here's to you, Ian. Happy camping.

◀ FOR 4

250G CHORIZO, CUT INTO CHUNKS
12 TBSP (ABOUT 300G) COOKED DICED POTATO – EQUIVALENT TO 2 MEDIUM SPUDS
6 LARGE EGGS
6 TBSP GRATED MATURE CHEDDAR
A PINCH OF FINELY CHOPPED CHILLI OR CHILLI FLAKES
4 LARGE TORTILLA WRAPS
2-3 TBSP CHOPPED CHIVES
A FEW SHAKES OF SPICY SAUCE (TRY HENDERSON'S RELISH, CHOLULA HOT SAUCE OR TABASCO)

Preheat the grill. In a large frying pan, sauté the chunks of chorizo until the oil begins to seep out and they begin to turn crispy. Then add the diced cooked potato (this is a good way to use up spuds from the previous night).

Cook over a medium high heat, stirring often, until the potatoes are hot and are beginning to go a little crispy. Then crack the eggs into the pan and scatter over the grated cheese and the chilli – stir well to break the eggs and create a kind of omelette. Heat the tortilla wraps under the grill.

Once the cheese has melted, sprinkle on the chopped chives. Then tip out the contents of the pan onto the warmed tortillas and add spicy sauce, to taste. Tuck in the ends and sides of the tortillas to make burritos and tuck in. You might need both hands.

parasol mushroom and
ROCK SAMPHIRE OMELETTE

This is a real forager's supper. Of course you can substitute shop-bought mushies for the parasol mushroom, but do look out for rock samphire with its lemony coastal flavour. It grows all around the coast.

◄ FOR 2

1 LARGE PARASOL MUSHROOM CAP, CUT INTO SLICES
OLIVE OIL, FOR FRYING
3-4 LARGE EGGS
HANDFUL FRESHLY PICKED, ROUGHLY CHOPPED ROCK SAMPHIRE

Fry the parasol mushroom slices in olive oil in a frying pan and season them. When they are cooked, remove the pan from the heat, crack in the eggs and add a tablespoon of cold water and some seasoning. Beat the eggs lightly with a fork, then return the pan to the heat and when the omelette begins to cook around the edges, scatter the samphire over the top.

Once the omelette is cooked underneath but still runny on top, flip one half of the omelette over the filling to make an envelope. Then flip the whole thing over and cook for a further few minutes before sliding out of the pan and onto a warm plate.

french onion soup
WITH CHEESY CROUTES

Need a little *Je ne sais quoi* in yer van? Bring out the big guns with this super-warming favourite. Mais oui? *Mais oui!*

MAKES 2 GENEROUS BOWLFULS
2 TBSP SOFT BUTTER
3 ONIONS, THINLY SLICED
2 CLOVES GARLIC, CRUSHED
2 TSP SUGAR
100MLS WHITE WINE OR DRY SHERRY
600MLS WELL-FLAVOURED BEEF STOCK – USE TWO GOOD QUALITY STOCK CUBES
4 SLICES OF BAGUETTE
DIJON MUSTARD
HANDFUL GRATED GRUYÈRE (OR CHEDDAR) CHEESE

Heat the butter in a medium pan until sizzling. Stir in the onions, garlic, sugar and a pinch of salt and cook over a low heat for 20-25 minutes or until the onions are meltingly soft and caramelised – stir them from time to time. Preheat the grill.

Turn up the heat in the pan and pour in the wine or sherry, bubble the liquid for a few minutes then add the stock and bring the soup back to simmering point. Meanwhile, toast the slices of baguette under the grill before generously spreading one side of each with mustard and topping with cheese, pressing it down to make it stick. Grill the croutes for a few minutes until melted and bubbling.

Ladle the soup into deep bowls and float two cheesy croutes on top of each one.

celeriac, crispy bacon and
PARSLEY COUSCOUS RISOTTO

Giant couscous makes a fine, albeit different, kind of risotto. It is also quicker to cook than rice. For a delicious vegetarian risotto, you can leave out the bacon and add a generous handful of toasted nuts at the end.

FOR 4

1 TBSP OLIVE OIL
8 RASHERS OF BACON, CHOPPED
800MLS HOT VEGETABLE OR CHICKEN STOCK
1 FAT CLOVE GARLIC, FINELY CHOPPED
300G PACK GIANT COUSCOUS (TRY MERCHANT GOURMET)
HALF A CELERIAC (ABOUT 300G), PEELED AND GRATED
2 TBSP BUTTER
2 GENEROUS HANDFULS GRATED CHEDDAR
SMALL BUNCH OF PARSLEY, STALKS DISCARDED, LEAVES CHOPPED

Heat the oil in a medium pan and fry the bacon for 6-7 minutes until crispy, then remove to a plate. Drain off and discard the fat from the pan, add the stock and garlic and bring to simmering point.

Tip in the couscous and celeriac and bring to boiling point. Reduce the heat and simmer for 7-8 minutes or until the couscous is tender – stir from time to time and add a dash more stock or hot water if you think it needs it.

Stir in most of the crispy bacon, the butter, grated Cheddar and parsley and season to taste. Spoon into bowls, top with the rest of the bacon and eat as soon as you can.

camper van
STEAK AND CHIPS

Give me a good, old-fashioned, down-to-earth piece of steak and I am a happy man. Add some chips and you've got a classic in the making. So you've got no deep fat fryer? It's no bad thing. Do it the camper van way.

FOR 2

3 LARGE POTATOES, SUCH AS KING EDWARDS

OIL, FOR FRYING

2 RIBEYE STEAKS

SMALL KNOB OF BUTTER

1 CLOVE GARLIC, FINELY CHOPPED

SMALL HANDFUL PARSLEY, CHOPPED

Peel and halve the potatoes then put them in salted water in a medium-sized pan. Bring to the boil and simmer for 3 minutes (you want them to be parboiled), then drain and cool before cutting into ½-¾ cm slices.

Heat 2-3 cms deep of oil in the cleaned pan (a deep-sided frying pan is ideal) and fry the 'chips' in two or three batches till golden. They will take 10-15 minutes, turning them halfway through cooking. Keep them warm as they are ready, under the grill maybe if your van has one.

To cook the steaks, heat a splash of oil and a knob of butter in a frying pan and when really hot, season the steaks and cook them for 2-3 minutes on each side until browned but still pink inside – baste them with the hot fat as they cook. Mix the garlic, parsley and some crushed sea salt, toss with the chips and serve with the steaks.

NOTE: Be careful with large quantities of hot oil in the van. Once you have finished with it, let it cool a little and then pour it into an empty jam jar and keep until the next time. Otherwise dispose of it responsibly.

AUBERGINE and mushroom curry

This is one that you might just need to plan ahead for. Some of the ingredients may be harder to find. But they won't take up too much room, so buy them in advance and stick them at the back of the cupboard.

This is also delicious with fried paneer cheese. Either way, some naan bread or rice is essential.

FOR 4

VEGETABLE OIL, FOR FRYING
1 TBSP BLACK MUSTARD SEEDS
1 TBSP BLACK ONION SEEDS
1 ONION, FINELY SLICED
3 CLOVES GARLIC, CRUSHED
3 CM PIECE OF ROOT GINGER, GRATED
1 TSP CRUSHED DRIED CHILLIES
1 MEDIUM AUBERGINE, TRIMMED AND CUT INTO SMALL CHUNKS
5 HANDFULS (250G) THICKLY SLICED CHESTNUT MUSHROOMS
2 X 400G TINS CHOPPED TOMATOES
1 TSP SUGAR
1 TBSP GARAM MASALA
1 TBSP TAMARIND PASTE
GREEK YOGHURT AND A HANDFUL OF CHOPPED CORIANDER LEAVES, TO SERVE

Heat two tablespoons of oil in a medium-sized pan, add the mustard seeds and onion seeds and gently heat. Once you hear these crackle and pop, stir in the sliced onion, garlic, ginger and dried chillies. Fry over a lowish heat for 8-10 minutes, stirring now and then, until the onions have softened.

Meanwhile, in a frying pan heat two more tablespoons of oil and fry the aubergine and mushrooms, in two batches, over a medium to high heat until softened and browned – add more oil as you need it.

Tip the vegetables into the pan to join the onions. Add the tomatoes and stir in the sugar. Bring everything to the boil then reduce the heat and simmer, covered, for 10 minutes.

Stir in the garam masala, tamarind paste and a generous seasoning of salt, simmer for a further few minutes. Spoon into bowls and top with yoghurt and coriander.

SEAFOOD LAKSA, for a crowd

This mild creamy soupy curry is based on a traditional Malaysian laksa. Vary the fish according to your catch or local fishmonger. If you want to soak the noodles ahead, toss them with a little oil, once drained, to prevent them sticking together.

FOR 8

3 HANDFULS (150G) SHELLED MACADAMIA NUT HALVES
2 TBSP OIL
285G JAR MEDIUM LAKSA CURRY PASTE (BLUE DRAGON OR SIMILAR)
4 X 400ML TINS COCONUT MILK
HALF A CUCUMBER
900G RICE NOODLES
FOUR HANDFULS (300G) BEANSPROUTS
JUICE OF 2 LIMES, PLUS WEDGES
4 HANDFULS (400G) SHELLED RAW PRAWNS
1KG SKINLESS WHITE FISH FILLET, CUT INTO CHUNKS
4 DOUBLE HANDFULS (1KG) MUSSELS, SCRUBBED AND BEARDS REMOVED
SMALL BUNCH OF MINT AND A BUNCH OF BASIL, LEAVES SHREDDED

First, toast the macadamias in a frying pan and when they are tinged golden, tip them onto a plate. Next, heat the oil in a large pan and add the curry paste, stir over the heat for a couple of minutes before adding the coconut milk. Slowly bring the liquid to simmering point.

Meanwhile, slice the cucumber into thick matchsticks (no need to peel) and put the noodles into a bowl, cover with boiling water and leave them to soak for 15 minutes or according to the pack instructions.

Stir the beansprouts, lime juice, prawns, fish, mussels and half a teaspoon of salt into the coconut milk in the pan. Simmer, uncovered, for 3-5 minutes until the fish is cooked and the mussels have opened (discard any closed shells). Stir in half the shredded herbs and mix the remaining with the nuts. Taste to check the seasoning.

Drain the noodles and divide them and the cucumber between eight deep bowls, ladle the laksa on top and sprinkle each one with the mixed herbs and nuts. Serve with lime wedges.

massaman chicken curry
WITH BEANS AND CASHEWS

A mild Thai curry to serve with rice and maybe some mango chutney or Indian pickle.
This recipe works great with a whole roast chicken, but if you find that hard to get hold
of, simply substitute four raw chicken breasts, which you should dice into chunks and
fry off beforehand.

FOR 4

1 WHOLE ROAST CHICKEN (ABOUT 1KG)
1 TBSP VEGETABLE OIL
2 TBSP MASSAMAN THAI CURRY PASTE (BART'S OR SIMILAR)
8 SMALL NEW POTATOES (250G), THICKLY SLICED
A COUPLE OF BAY LEAVES
A CINNAMON STICK
500MLS HOT CHICKEN STOCK
200ML CARTON COCONUT CREAM
1 GENEROUS HANDFUL FINE GREEN BEANS, CUT INTO SHORT LENGTHS
HANDFUL CASHEW NUTS
3 TBSP CHOPPED CORIANDER

Joint the roast chicken and cut the meat into chunks, discarding the skin and bones.
Heat the oil in a medium-sized pan and stir in the paste, cook for a minute, stirring. Add
the potatoes, bay leaves, cinnamon stick and stock and bring to the boil, then gently
simmer, uncovered, for 10 minutes.

Stir in the chicken, coconut cream and beans. Bring the curry back to simmering
point and simmer, covered, over a low heat for 10-15 minutes or till the potatoes are
tender. Add salt to taste and finally stir in the cashews and coriander.

pork, scrumpy, apple AND FENNEL POT ROAST

Fancy a little scrumping? Do it! Just don't get caught. It'll make you feel like a schoolboy again, complete with grazed knees and sticky-out ears. Served with a mustard and horseradish mash, this is the perfect dish for a Sunday night in September.

◀ FOR 4

2 RED ONIONS	VEGETABLE OIL, FOR FRYING
2 CLOVES GARLIC	ABOUT 500MLS SCRUMPY (OR ORGANIC CIDER)
3 EATING APPLES	BAY LEAF
1 MEDIUM BULB FENNEL	A FEW SPRIGS OF LEMON THYME
500G PORK FILLET	2 TSP CORNFLOUR, IF YOU LIKE, SEE BELOW

First, peel and quarter the onions, peel and halve the garlic cloves, core and thickly slice the apples and trim and quarter the fennel.

Next, season the pork fillet all over. Then heat a casserole (or Dutch oven) with a little vegetable oil and when sizzling, brown the pork fillet all over, turning it as you do so.

Remove the pork to a plate and pour a little scrumpy into the casserole. Let the cider bubble away for a minute or so, then add the onions, garlic and bay leaf. Cook briefly for a few minutes to begin to soften the onions, adding a little oil if the cider evaporates, then place the browned pork fillet on top.

Scatter the fennel, apple slices and sprigs of thyme around the pork. Pour in the rest of the scrumpy, it should more or less cover the vegetables, then bring the whole thing to the boil. Once the liquid is boiling, put a lid on and reduce the heat. Leave the pork to simmer slowly on the hob for 25-30 minutes or until the pork is cooked through.

When the time is up, remove the fillet from the casserole and slice it thickly, then serve with the apple and fennel and the scrumpy. If you prefer a thicker sauce, mix the cornflour with 2-3 teaspoons of cold water in a cup and when you have removed the pork from the casserole, stir the cornflour mixture into the hot scrumpy over the heat and simmer briefly to thicken.

cocktail for autumn –
BLACKBERRY LIME FIZZ

FOR 6
3 JUICY LIMES
3 TBSP CASTER SUGAR
CRÈME DE CASSIS OR CRÈME DE MURE
1 BOTTLE PROSECCO, CHILLED
BLACKBERRIES, TO FINISH

Squeeze the limes, then strain and mix with the sugar. Put a sixth into each of six glasses, followed by a dash or two of crème de cassis or crème de mure. Top up with Prosecco and add a blackberry or two to each one.

A TEA FOR THE AUTUMN: Chamomile tea*
Chamomile is another of those teas that you can pick wild if you can find it. It flowers until late summer and is one of the most effective medicinal teas known. Great for insomnia, sore throats and, taken at regular intervals, used to 'cure' colds.

MAKING THE PERFECT CUPPA
Place 2 to 4 teaspoons of fresh or dried flowers per cup into a teapot. Pour on boiled water and steep for three minutes. Strain and serve. Sweeten with local honey, if you like.

* avoid if pregnant.

WINTER

Cold starts, woolly hats and wild seas

When our kids Maggie and Charlie were tiny we had a T25 with a gas-powered heater. It even had a thermostat that you could set to whatever temperature you liked. It meant that we could park up at the beach near our house and spend the entire day cooking, reading and taking it easy — in a beautifully cosy van — when all around was blowing and cold and miserable. If there was a break in the cloud we'd rush outside to make the most of the fresh winter air. And when the rain came down again we'd retreat to the warmth of our cocoon on wheels, put the kettle on, grab a slice of home-made cake and thank our lucky stars we weren't stuck inside the house with nothing to do.

That's winter. It's a time for snatching precious moments out of the gloom, of bright sunny mornings and long nights, of howling winds and breathless walks. It's a time of raging seas and chilly toes. But it can also be a time for eating well. Warming, spicy stews provide fuel for frosty days out, whilst a classic camper van curry will keep anyone's sprits up during an Arctic-like surf trip.

Winter is also a time for getting out. Turn a trip into the cold into a trip with a purpose by gathering a few mussels from the beach. Nip out to get some winter vegetables for an earthy bowl of winter crisps (page 267). Once out there you can marvel at the work of nature on the once-calm seascapes, now virtually unrecognisable from the summertime. A visit to a lighthouse will remind you why you aren't on a boat at this time of year. And there's always a pub to dash into if the weather goes bad.

For the diehards, winter isn't a time for being stopped in your tracks at all, as long as you know what you're doing. Waking up to snow is quite wonderful if you've got enough togs to keep you warm and a few slices of black pudding to pop under the grill. And so you might need to drive away in mittens and a scarf and you might not be able to see out of the windscreen for the first half an hour of your journey. But so what? You take the rough with the smooth.

And besides, there's still Christmas dinner to look forward to.

It won't cook itself you know

Camping into winter

I've woken up to snow a few times whilst camping and it really is quite magical, but I wouldn't want to do it all the time. It takes a special kind of camper to brave a trip in the depths of winter. To do it, you'll need to be prepared.

Don't forget your season-specific sleeping bag (see page 25) and your long johns. It might also be a good idea to take a little look at this list. It could save your bacon. In the case of the type of gas you use, that means literally.

BATTERIES The optimum working temperature for a lead acid battery is 25°C. Performance drops considerably in cold temperatures, which is problematic in the winter, when you need more light and power to keep warm and amused.

If power for your lights and heat comes from the main vehicle battery (which is designed to give a high current output for short bursts), you could lose the oomph to crank up the engine in the morning. Leisure batteries provide a low current for long periods of time, so are ideal for powering lights, radios, phone chargers and so on. They also leave the main battery free to start the van. If your camper has electric hookup you might also want to consider fitting a mains-powered battery charger.

In lots of campers the batteries are outside the van, in the engine compartment. Others, like the T25, host the batteries under the seats in front. All lead acid batteries vent hydrogen (an explosive gas) as part of their normal working chemical reaction, so batteries inside your van should be housed in a container, which is sealed off from the living space, but vented to the outside.

ON-BOARD HEATING Campers of the VW variety are notorious for having poor heating. There are things you can do to improve this:

Original heat exchangers are more efficient than the majority of aftermarket heat exchangers, so if you can find some, it's worth paying a little extra to have them fitted.

Insulation will also help. Make sure the ducts that deliver heat to the cab are still insulated and that all the connectors, cables and joints are working properly.

ADDITIONAL HEATING If you stay on sites with electric hookup then small plug-in heaters are perfect for a camper. But if you want to go off-piste (and I hope you do) then you'll need a self-contained heating system that's safe and warm, come what may. The most common option is a warm, blown air heater that's fuelled by LPG (propane or butane) or by the vehicle fuel (petrol or diesel). 'Room sealed' heaters are recommended for safety (especially if you're going to use the heater overnight), but it's always a good idea to carry an audible carbon monoxide alarm.

NOTE: Don't ever use the burners on a gas stove to keep warm. Prolonged use of a stove inside a closed camper van will gradually reduce the oxygen content of the air and then start to produce carbon monoxide, risking suffocation and gas poisoning.

COOKING WITH GAS There are two types of gas you can use for your cooker and fridge: propane and butane. Butane is popular for summer use as it has the higher calorific value (i.e. it boils the kettle faster than propane), but it stops vaporising at around -1°C, which causes reduced gas pressure. Not what you need on a frosty morning! Propane continues to vaporise at -42°C, so your gas appliances should perform effectively whatever the weather.

INSULATION The general rule here is to allow for adequate ventilation: be sure not to block any fixed vents and seek advice if you need it.

UNDER FLOOR A plywood and expanded foam sandwich works if you're building a van from scratch. Otherwise use carpet or rugs for additional warmth.

INSIDE PANELS Gaps between the interior trim panels and the external bodywork can be filled with standard loft insulation, sheep's wool, or multi-layered foil. Make sure any moisture-retaining materials are self-contained or they could cause rust and rot.

BARE METAL SURFACES You lose a lot of heat here. Cover using soft material that can be worked into contours of the bodywork.

WINDOWS Silver insulating screens with suction cups are available to fit most camper vans. Alternatively, make your own from air cell insulation or even bubble wrap.

HI-TOP ROOFS You may be able to install additional headlining boards with insulation behind, or fasten removable sections of air cell with Velcro.

ELEVATING ROOFS Canvas side panels are breathable and so insulating these with non-breathable material risks condensation.

WATER Frozen water systems are a major problem for winter camper vanners, because it can damage pipes, joints, taps and pumps when it freezes. By far the cheapest way round this is to drain your water tank at the start of winter and simply use a jerry can inside the van for your water.

STAYING PRETTY

Winter is a harsh time for old vehicles. Many of the earliest campers won't have galvanised panels and will have minimal rust proofing. That means that you'll need to take a little extra care if you intend to drive right through and don't want the van to disintegrate before your eyes. Even if you don't intend to camp through the winter, there are still a few things to think about.

★ Road salt is lethal for old vehicles because it's so corrosive. So avoid driving when it's been put on the roads. If you do have to drive when salt is down, wash the van underneath with fresh water.

★ Waxoyl the underneath of your van to protect from water ingress and corrosion. Clean off the underneath of the van with a wire brush before applying.

★ Fit mudguards to the van. This will prevent spray from mud, stones and road salt and help to avoid stone chips which cause corrosion.

★ Keep the van clean and wax regularly to stop the paintwork getting dull/corroding.

★ Make sure the van is mechanically sound. You don't want to break down when it's wet and cold.

PUTTING THE VAN INTO WINTER STORAGE

If you can't face the prospect of rust and rot setting in, then you might want to consider putting your van into winter storage. Lots of owners will let their cherished campers hibernate over the cold months. It's not a bad idea. The winter can take its toll on any vehicle. So, you want it to stay beautiful. A few simple rules will make sure your baby steps into the spring sunshine as sweet as it was the day you left it.

★ Dry spaces with good ventilation are perfect for storing vehicles. Barns are good, garages equally so. If you can't find somewhere dry, consider buying a vehicle cover. They cost about £100 from www.justkampers.com.

★ If you are planning on storing your van in one of Ian's barns at SW Classic VWs (www.southwestvws.co.uk) then don't leave any beer in the fridge. It will get drunk. Guaranteed. It's happened before and it'll happen again.

★ Similarly, don't leave any food in the van anywhere. Mice will find it. They also eat bedding and wiring and anything else that a mouse considers tasty.

★ Disconnect the battery and take it out of the van. Charge it up once a month to make sure it keeps in good condition. Leisure batteries don't like being run down so make sure you top that up too.

★ Start the engine once a month and run it for 30 minutes or so. If you can and it's dry, take it out for a run. At the very least, drive it a few feet to make sure nothing has seized.

★ Check the tyre pressure and make sure there isn't a slow puncture. Tyres that bulge will disintegrate quickly.

★ Leave the hand brake off to avoid the brakes rusting on. If they do, hit them with a rubber mallet to free them before driving off (driving off will often free them anyway). If you leave the handbrake off, leave the van in gear and chock the wheels.

★ Tell the DVLA that your vehicle is off the road (SORN).

Hitting the road

OK. So you're one of the brave ones who like to use the van for what it's meant to be used for. That's hitting the road, at any time of the year. So go see some stuff…

Have you ever wondered what it feels like to be the last person alive on earth? You can get pretty near to it on a windy winter's day at the coast. Just take a walk along the prom at about four o'clock on a Tuesday afternoon and see what it's like. Imagine you are the only one left (apart from the couple snogging in the bus shelter) and see how you feel. Is it liberating to be the only one there, save the gulls?

Any old seaside resort will do, preferably one with a population of less than 5,000 people.

Spooky

See the power

If there's one thing that is sure to make you feel inferior in the depths of a winter storm, it's the sea. But to have the chance to watch grown men and women ride waves of up to 40 or 50 feet is a rare and precious spectacle indeed. If you witness it you might then want to go and pop a penny in the lifeboat. You know, just in case (see page 252).

ATLANTIC MONSTERS: Tow surfing in the big waves

One of the beneficial side effects of winter in the Northern Hemisphere is the ability of the North Atlantic Ocean to deliver huge low pressure systems – and massive waves – to the west facing coasts of Britain and Ireland. There are only a few places around our coast that will have waves of any consequential size to big wave surfers. And by 'consequential', I don't mean a bit too big to go for a paddle, I mean HUGE. Over 20 feet could probably qualify, although waves of twice that size are surfed regularly off Ireland's west coast.

Andrew Cotton from North Devon, together with his surfing partner Al Mennie, is one of a handful surfing the biggest waves that break upon our shores. They have been photographed surfing waves of up to 50 feet on the face. Waves so big that they cannot catch them by paddling in the normal way and have to be towed into them using a PWC (personal water craft), letting go of the tow rope at the last minute. Experienced PWC drivers put their surfers into very large waves and get them out again if they fall.

Why?

Surfing is addictive and yet also very elusive. I don't know any surfer who had such a good day at the beach that they were ready to hang up their wetsuit. There is always more to take on. Tow surfing, as far as I see it, is about pushing limits, getting a bigger buzz. But it's also about finding new places to surf and getting away from the crowds. What better than surfing huge waves with a few friends whilst the world looks on in awe?

BEST SEAT IN THE HOUSE

If you fancy seeing what all the fuss is about, find out from local surf shops where the best vantage points are. Keep an eye on surf forecast sites for the right conditions like www.magicseaweed.com. Swell of over 2 metres with light local winds is a good start. These are the UK's top spots:

THE CRIBBAR, North Cornwall

The site of England's first big wave contest. Breaks on a shallow reef off Towan Head, to the north of Fistral Beach. Watch from the headland.

OYSTERS, North Devon

A 'big wave' spot that breaks about a quarter of a mile from Croyde Bay. Tackled by mad men and adrenaline junkies.

AILEEN'S, County Clare

At the foot of the very terrifying Cliffs of Moher. One of the world's best 'big wave' spots, it has a top viewing spot: from the top of the cliffs themselves.

MULLAGHMORE, Sligo

Another terrifying Irish monster that's helping to put Ireland on the world map of surfing all over again. Top views from Mullaghmore Head.

Thinking about having a go?

There is nothing to stop you from launching a jet ski and giving it a pop. All you have to do is want it badly enough and not mind the consequences. Having said that, don't. It's a really bad idea.

★ You don't need a licence but it's advisable to take a K38 Water Safety course (www.h2osafety.co.uk): an internationally recognised certificate in PWC competency.

★ You don't need insurance to own a jet ski but many slipways and councils won't let you launch without it.

★ The Yamaha Wave Runner 1200 is the big wave rider's vehicle of choice. It retails at about £7,000.

★ Andrew and Al took the best part of a year learning the ropes. Take your time. And maybe, just maybe...

Top lifeboat stations

The RNLI are a vital part of our coast. If you ever get into trouble out on the sea, they are the people who will come and do all they can to make it better. They are a very brave bunch of lads and lasses who put themselves in danger so that others may live. And many of them are volunteers. As a surfer, I have the utmost respect for what they do.

RNLI Explore Stations are open to visitors all year round. That means you can pop along and have a gander at the boats, make a donation, buy a few trinkets in the gift shop and meet some of the crew who man them. Take time to ask a few questions and you might hear some remarkable stories. With 235 lifeboat stations covering our coasts, you won't have to go far out of your way to appreciate the work they do.

The UK's best lifeboat stations

MOST DECORATED: Cromer, Norfolk An Explore Station whose crew included the RNLI's Henry George Blogg. He carried out 154 rescues and saved 448 lives on the HF Bailey boat over its 10-year service in Cromer.

BUSIEST: Poole, Dorset In 2009 this RNLI lifeboat station launched 200 times.

MOST SOUTHERLY: The Lizard, Cornwall There have been RNLI lifeboats at the Lizard since 1859. Covering one of the busiest shipping lanes in the world, it is now home to a brand new station.

BEST LOVED: Moelfre, Anglesey An Explore Station with a statue to Dic Evans, ex-coxswain, who was awarded gold a medal in 1959 after service in hurricane winds. Nearly 10,000 attended the station open day in 2010.

PRETTIEST: St Davids, Pembrokeshire Another remote station that's set up for a super-fast launch.

OLDEST: Sunderland, Tyne and Wear The oldest lifeboat station, celebrating over 200 years. The first motor lifeboat in the RNLI's fleet operated from here.

MOST READY: The Humber, East Riding of Yorkshire The only lifeboat station with a full-time crew, based on Spurn Point.

MOST NORTHERLY: Aith, Orkney Islands The most northerly lifeboat station providing protection for mariners off Shetland's Atlantic coast.

BEST LOCATION: Tobermory, Argyll and Bute, Isle of Mull You'll find this explore station in Tobermory, the oh-so-cute town on Mull that doubled for Balamory in the BBC children's TV show.

YOUNGEST: Kinsale, County Cork Situated on the picturesque south west coast of Ireland, Kinsale is one of the newest RNLI lifeboat stations.

RNLI Lifeguards run more than 150 lifeguard stations at beaches around the UK. You might think of this lot as the Baywatch crew (although often better looking and fitter) but don't be put off by the shades and the shorts. These are the people who save lives on our beaches. And they don't do it by running in slow motion either. Every year lifeguards save more than 60 lives and assist almost 10,000 people who have got into difficulties. Read all about it at **www.rnli.org.uk**

Go See Some art

I'm an art lover. And I especially love public art. At one level it brightens up the place and shows that we care about our environment, but on another level it can make us ask questions, remember important events, show us the way or teach us hard-learned lessons. I like to be challenged and inspired by art, whether it's by my idea of what art is or by deeper questions.

We are lucky enough in the UK and Ireland to have some stunning works of public art on our coastline. Some, like Anthony Gormley's 'Another Place' at Crosby Beach or the 'Time and Tide Bell' by Marcus Vergette at Appledore, change with the ebb and flow of the earth's natural rhythms. Others, like Sam Holland's RNLI memorial sculpture in Poole, serve as a poignant reminder of the perils of the sea and the heroism of those who volunteer.

ART INSTALLATIONS

The north

ANOTHER PLACE by Anthony Gormley
A haunting collection of 100 cast-iron sculptures, replicas of Anthony Gormley's body, on Crosby Beach, Merseyside.

BATHING BEAUTIES by various artists
A series of unique artist-inspired beach huts on the Lincolnshire Coast between Mablethorpe and Anderby Creek.

COUPLE by Sean Henry
A huge couple looking out to sea at Newbiggin Bay, Northumberland.

TEMENOS by Anish Kapoor and Cecil Balmond
A 50-metre high, 100-metre long structure on Middlesbrough dock. The first of five huge sculptures planned for the region as part of the Tees Valley Giants public art project. Impressive stuff.

THE TERN PROJECT by various artists
A collection of artworks along the central promenade at Morecambe. Includes a statue of Eric Morecambe and bird bollards.

The south

PASSACAGLIA by Charles Hadcock
One of Brighton's most photographed landmarks, Hadcock's large curved cast-iron sculpture in the form of a tile tessellation, was inspired by limestone terraces at Black Head in Ireland.

SCALLOP by Maggi Hambling
Rising out of the shingle of Aldeburgh beach, Hambling's beautiful shells are a tribute to local son Benjamin Britten, inscribed with words from his opera *Peter Grimes.*

FULL FATHOM FIVE by Michael Dan Archer
This is what coastal art should be. One of the UK's biggest installations, it comprises 108 granite pillars on a hillside in Portishead, Bristol. Striking, thoughtful, inspiring.

TIME AND TIDE BELL PROJECT by Marcus Vergette

Vergette is planning to install 12 bells around the UK, rung by the sea at high tide. The first, at Appledore, North Devon, is inspired. On high tides expect a higher pitch. With rising sea levels expect a cacophony.

THE MINEHEAD MARKER by Sarah Ward

A big old pair of hands holding open a big old map. Marks the start of the South West Coast Path. Nice touch.

Scotland

TAIGH CHEARSABGHAGH MUSEUM AND ARTS CENTRE

Lochmaddy, Uist. Gallery with strong local and community ties on the edge of the world.

THE MERMAID OF THE NORTH by Stephen Hayward

A lovely mermaid sits on a rock and tempts you in. I would. Part of the Seaboard Sculpture Trail.

Wales

STEEL WAVE by Peter Fink

Fourteen metres high and made from 50 tonnes of steel, this is Newport's striking reminder of our seafaring and industrial past.

MERCHANT SEAFARERS' WAR MEMORIAL by Brian Fell

Cardiff Bay's emotional and surprising memorial to those lost at sea.

Ireland

FLYING ANGEL by Maurice Harron

Here to watch over us, a modern steel symbol of the seafarers' mission. Princes Dock Street, Belfast.

THE FISHING BOAT by Niall O'Neill

Bronze sculpture on Portstewart Prom, erected to commemorate the life and work of local songwriter Jimmy Kennedy, genius behind 'Red Sails in the Sunset' and many more.

VOYAGER by Linda Brunker

A beautiful sculpture on Laytown seafront in Meath. Much loved and incredibly enigmatic.

Roosting starlings at dusk

If you've never seen a 'murmuration' of starlings in the November skies, then it's reason enough to head out at dusk. This is one of our most mesmerising winter spectacles. In choosing their collective roost for the night, starlings gather in enormous numbers, flying in flocks of thousands, sometimes even tens of thousands.

The flock moves as one, like a cloud of black dots, changing direction in an instant, creating ever-evolving shapes against the early evening sky. We've seen birds of prey dart among them, scattering the flock and creating tumbling, twisting, turning shapes as each bird evades capture.

According to the RSPB, loss of habitat, a shortage of food and roosting sites and a change in farming methods are causing the starling population to decline rapidly (by around 70% in recent years), so get out and try to see this wonderful show before it's too late.

Starlings roost all over the countryside, but Gretna Green in Dumfries and Galloway, and Brighton Pier, Sussex, are earmarked as top spots by the RSPB. Or visit an RSPB reserve, such as Leighton Moss, Lancashire; Saltholme, Middlesbrough; Ham Wall, Somerset; Newport Wetlands, Newport; or Snape, Suffolk to witness this truly epic natural event.

Roasting chestnuts on a beach fire

You know that Christmas is coming when chestnuts come into season. If you're lucky enough to gather a crop for yourself then you're in for a treat, but if you can't find any in the wild then a quick foray to the greengrocer's should yield at least a bag or two. In any case, getting your hands on some chestnuts is a good excuse to light up a beach fire and give them a jolly good roasting. And it's dead easy. Another one of those simple but great pleasures. Happily they taste lovely. It turns out that Bob the Dog loves them too, so beware.

The traditional way to roast chestnuts over a fire is to use a special iron frying pan with holes in it. These are designed to let the flames give the chestnuts a gentle lick as they cook. To carry one in your van, or even to buy one in the first place, is a little extravagant (unless you can't live without your daily roast chestnuts). A good heavy skillet will work just as well.

The secret to making pretty (and easy to peel) chestnuts is to nick an X into the pointy bit with a sharp knife. This will also stop them exploding, as the steam will be able to escape as they heat up. We can do without exploding nuts, thanks.

Roasting takes about 10-15 minutes over a medium hot beach fire made with driftwood. And don't forget that they will be hot, so wait a few minutes before peeling them. A little pinch of sea salt will add to the taste.

Visit a lighthouse

If ever there was an icon it is the red and white striped lighthouse sitting on the cliff top, silently safeguarding seafarers as they go about their dangerous business. But have you ever wondered what it would be like to live in one? What about one clinging to a rock in the middle of the ocean?

There are hundreds of lighthouses around the coast but only a handful that are open to the public. If you choose to go during a storm, when day seems like night and the spray hisses up from the churning sea as it slaps and crashes against the rocks, then you might glimpse how difficult life must have been for the people charged with keeping the light shining. It's no wonder there are so many stories of lighthouse keepers going a bit mad.

Today the lights are electrified and automated and operated by some bloke in a darkened room (probably but not definitely). But even so, every penny that you spend visiting one of our spectacular lighthouses will help to keep the lights on, even if nobody is home.

One of my favourites is Smeaton's Tower in Plymouth. It first shone its light over the ocean in October 1759 at Eddystone Rock, 15 miles offshore. Shortly thereafter, the top third of it was moved, block by block, to Plymouth when it was discovered that the rock upon which it was built was eroding. Take a look around. Imagine being stuck inside that for three months at a time.

Trinity House (www.trinityhouse.co.uk) has been responsible for many of our

lighthouses since the 17th century. They operate visitor centres at 11 lighthouses in England and Wales. There are also a handful of lighthouses with visitor centres around Scotland (www.nlb.org.uk) and Ireland (www.commissionersofirishlights.com). Check visiting hours and book first.

Lighthouse list

1 THE OLDEST OPERATIONAL LIGHT:
Hook Head, County Wexford
A 13th-century Norman structure. Built by monks, first powered by coal and now open as a visitor attraction.

3 MOST ROMANTIC:
Nash Point, South Glamorgan
The only lighthouse that's licensed for weddings and civil ceremonies; take the bus for a spin, end up getting carried away.

5 OLDEST LIGHT LOCATION:
St Catherine's, Isle of Wight
A light was established here in 1323. That's remarkable. It's also got an octagonal tower.

7 LEAST ISOLATED:
Southwold, Suffolk
It's in the middle of the town. Odd but great. Not far to walk.

9 THE MOST WESTERLY:
Ardnamurchan, Scottish Highlands
It's a widdly road to get there but the views over the Hebrides are amazing.

2 THE MOST SOUTHERLY:
Lizard Point, Cornwall
Visitor centre, fog horns, play areas: the lot. Looks a bit like a castle.

4 MOST LIKE A LIGHTHOUSE:
Portland Bill, Dorset
With a big red stripe and a visitor centre.

6 BEST BIRD WATCHING:
South Stack, Isle of Anglesey
Set in an RSPB reserve, South Stack is an exciting trip all right. You descend 400 steps to get to the bridge to get to the island to get to the lighthouse.

8 THE TALLEST:
North Ronaldsay, Orkney Islands
Planning an island-hopping adventure? Hop here! At 139 feet, it's the tallest land-based lighthouse in the British Isles.

10 THE FIRST SCOTTISH LIGHTHOUSE:
Fraserburgh, Aberdeenshire
The Kinnaird Head lighthouse was the first to be built on the Scottish mainland. It cast its light for the first time in December 1787. A visitor centre at the lighthouse museum houses a remarkable collection of lenses and equipment from Scottish lighthouses.

11 MOST ICONIC:
Beachy Head, Sussex
You can see this light from the cliffs but for the best view, take a boat. It's one of those views that shouts 'England' at you. White cliffs, red and white striped lighthouse, blue sea.

12 SMALLEST, HIGHEST AND DEEPEST:
Berry Head, Devon
It's only a few metres tall but high on a big cliff. The light used to be turned by the action of a weight falling down a 45-metre shaft.

13 MOST ROBUST:
Orfordness, Suffolk
This lighthouse has survived all kinds of stuff: plane crashes, wars, invasions and terrible weather. It's pretty too.

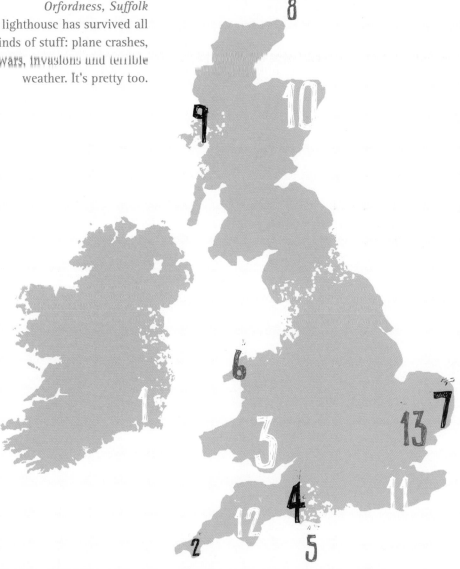

Sometimes a little spice to steam up the window in your camper is all you need to see you through. That's when the humble curry comes into its own. In fact, anything with a bite will help to bring the colour back to your cheeks. It's winter. Give yourself a little TLC.

standby CORNED BEEF HASH

Now this is camping. But then again it isn't. And that's because this is a corned beef hash recipe with a difference. Perfect for a winter brekkie.

FOR 2, GENEROUSLY
3 TBSP OIL
2 MEDIUM ONIONS, FINELY SLICED
1 CLOVE GARLIC, FINELY CHOPPED
2 LARGE MAINCROP POTATOES (450G), CUT INTO SMALL CHUNKS (NO NEED TO PEEL)
340G TIN CORNED BEEF
1 TBSP GRAINY MUSTARD
1 TBSP WORCESTERSHIRE SAUCE, PLUS EXTRA TO SERVE
2 TOMATOES, CHOPPED
2 LARGE EGGS

Heat two tablespoons of the oil in a frying pan and fry the onions, over a low-medium heat, for about 10 minutes or until soft, adding the garlic halfway. At the same time, bring a pan of salted water to the boil and boil the potato chunks for 5 minutes, or until tender but still holding their shape.

Drain the potatoes and add them to the onions in the pan along with the corned beef, mustard, Worcestershire sauce and tomatoes. Toss everything together over a highish heat until piping hot.

Make two holes in the hash and break an egg into each. Season the eggs and put the pan under the grill to cook the eggs for 3-4 minutes or until set to your liking. (If the pan won't fit under the grill, fry the eggs separately.) Serve in the pan with extra Worcestershire sauce on the side to add as you eat.

WINTER veg crisps

'Oh no, it's another turnip!' says Joanne almost every Saturday morning when our veg box arrives during the depths of winter. 'What am I going to do with that?' It's a common problem in our house and one that we've had to solve by mashing, roasting, boiling and frying on more than one occasion. It hasn't always gone down well. Anyway, we've sorted it now by adding a few of our more favoured winter veg – the parsnip and the underrated beetroot – to come up with our 'super healthy bag of winter vegetable crisps with thyme and sea salt'. Because everyone loves crisps. Lineker would be proud. And it's remarkably easy to do. It goes like this …

◀ FOR 3-4
1 LARGE BEETROOT
1 LARGE PARSNIP
HALF A LARGE TURNIP
VEGETABLE OIL, FOR FRYING
SEA SALT AND DRIED THYME, FOR SPRINKLING

Peel the vegetables. Then use a flat-bladed vegetable peeler to slice the vegetables into very thin slices, as thin as you dare. If you do this across the grain then you'll get almost perfectly circular shapes for the beetroot and parsnip. You may find it easier to slice the turnip into thin strips. Pat the slices or strips dry with kitchen paper.

Heat up about half a centimetre of oil in a frying pan or saucepan over a high heat – test it with a small cube of bread, which should turn golden in seconds – you want it to be really hot. Fry one vegetable at a time and fry the slices in a single layer in the hot oil. Don't be tempted to put too many in at once, or you will end up with a clump more than a crisp.

Shake the pan from time to time, so the oil covers the crisps, and cook them until they start to turn golden – a matter of minutes. Remove the crisps from the oil as they are ready and transfer them to a sieve lined with kitchen paper to drain before tipping them onto a plate. When you have cooked the lot, sprinkle with crushed sea salt and dried thyme.

poor man's POTATOES

When I mentioned a little while ago to my friend Simon that I had discovered this traditional Spanish dish (it's known as Patatas a lo Pobre) he announced very casually that he used to cook it all the time on surf trips in his T25 to the west coast of France. So, it's a proven camper van favourite. And if you needed more proof of its compatibility with camper van life, a friend held a competition on her foodie blog for the very best cook-it-in-yer-camper-van recipe. Guess what won? You got it! A deluxe version of this recipe. This is the basic version but you can add all kinds of other lovely things to it like red peppers, herbs and perhaps even a smidge of cumin. YUM!

 FOR 2

1 LARGE ONION

OLIVE OIL (LOTS OF IT)

2 CLOVES GARLIC, FINELY CHOPPED

1 GREEN PEPPER, CORED AND SLICED

1 BAY LEAF

4 LARGE SPUDS, PEELED AND DICED

2 LARGE EGGS, IF YOU FANCY

Gently fry the onion in at least 3 tablespoons of olive oil, in a frying pan, until soft. Add the garlic, pepper and bay leaf and cook for 10 minutes over a low heat. Next, add the potatoes and some seasoning and follow this with enough olive oil, 4-5 tablespoons, to almost cover the potatoes. Cover the pan and simmer everything over a low heat for 15 minutes or until the potatoes are cooked and have begun to break up. Transfer to plates using a slotted spoon.

   If you want to add eggs, make a couple of indentations in the mixture a few minutes before the end of the cooking time and break the eggs into them. Continue to cook until the eggs are cooked to your liking.

lentils with sweet potato,
HARISSA AND TOASTED SEEDS

Red lentils are a curious thing as they trick you by turning orangey yellow when cooked. If you can, forage for sea beet and use it in place of the spinach.

FOR 3-4
200G RED LENTILS
1 ONION, CHOPPED
2 STICKS CELERY, CHOPPED
2 SMALL SWEET POTATOES (375G), PEELED AND CHOPPED
4 TSP CUMIN SEEDS
2 TBSP OIL
3 HANDFULS SPINACH, CHOPPED IF NOT YOUNG LEAF
3 TBSP BUTTER
2 TBSP PUMPKIN SEEDS
1 TBSP FINELY CHOPPED ROOT GINGER
1 CLOVE GARLIC, FINELY CHOPPED
SEA SALT FLAKES
HARISSA AND HANDFUL MINT LEAVES, SHREDDED, TO SERVE

Rinse the lentils in cold water in a sieve, then drain. In a medium-sized pan, fry the onion, celery, sweet potato and half of the cumin seeds in the oil for 10 minutes.

Stir in the lentils and 500mls cold water, bring to the boil and simmer briskly for 10-15 minutes, uncovered, or until both the lentils and potato are tender.

Add the spinach, one handful at a time to allow it to wilt. Stir in a third of the butter and season with salt – be generous, lentils like salt.

Melt the remaining butter in a frying pan and fry the rest of the cumin seeds, the pumpkin seeds, ginger, garlic and a sprinkle of sea salt flakes for 3-4 minutes.

Spoon the hot lentils into bowls. Top with a generous teaspoonful of harissa, mint and the toasted seeds.

MART'S CHORIZO and bean stew

This is one for those days when you're scrabbling around in the cupboard, can't find anything fresh and can't be bothered to go to the shops. It can be made entirely from tins and dried ingredients and the king of the long-stay staples, chorizo. You could even stash the tins at the back of the cupboard and then whip them out when the 'What's for tea?' gloom sets in.

If ever you were tempted to heat up a tin of peas, meat and potatoes (a classic camping horror known to some as 'holiday stew') and call it dinner, STOP! Make this instead. It's filling, it's easy, it's very rustic and it's great with chunky bread and butter. If you wanted to make it a thick and chunky broth, use double the amount of stock, whilst a little extra chilli wouldn't go amiss if you like it nicey spicey like that.

◀ FOR 4

OLIVE OIL AND KNOB OF BUTTER FOR FRYING

1 ONION, FINELY CHOPPED

1 CLOVE GARLIC

1 TBSP OREGANO, CHOPPED

1 TBSP THYME, CHOPPED

225G CHORIZO SAUSAGE, CHOPPED INTO CHUNKS ABOUT 2 CM SQUARE

400G TIN CHOPPED TOMATOES

400G TIN BUTTER BEANS

400G TIN KIDNEY BEANS

400G TIN CANNELLINI BEANS

200MLS BEEF STOCK (A BEEF STOCK CUBE WILL DO)

Melt the butter in a large pan. Add the olive oil and fry the onions over a gentle heat for 5 minutes until they are soft. Then add the garlic, the herbs and the chorizo. Cook for a further 2-3 minutes until the oils have come out of the chorizo. Add the tomatoes, the beans and the stock. Stir and bring slowly back to simmering point. Season well with salt and black pepper. Simmer for a further 15 minutes then serve.

lamb gosht CURRY

Camping and curry are age-old travelling companions. So, it seems only right to pay homage to the humble rogan josh with an easy version of our own. If you brew this up at a campsite you'll have your neighbours sniffing around in no time. So, chill enough of that fabulous Indian beer in the river… it could end up being a dinner party. Serve with quick chapattis (see page 274) or rice if you prefer.

◀ FOR 4

VEGETABLE OIL, FOR FRYING

1KG LEG OF LAMB, DICED

1 LARGE ONION, CHOPPED

2 CM PIECE OF ROOT GINGER, FINELY CHOPPED

2 LARGE CLOVES GARLIC, FINELY CHOPPED

1 RED CHILLI, FINELY CHOPPED
   (OR MORE IF YOU LIKE THINGS SPICY)

1 TSP GARAM MASALA, PLUS EXTRA TO SPRINKLE

1 TSP GROUND TURMERIC

1 TSP GROUND CORIANDER

400G TIN CHOPPED TOMATOES

A BIG SQUIRT OF TOMATO PURÉE

4 TOMATOES, ROUGHLY CHOPPED

GENEROUS HANDFUL BABY SPINACH
   LEAVES

HANDFUL CORIANDER LEAVES

SOURED CREAM, TO SERVE

Heat a saucepan with a dash of vegetable oil. Brown the lamb in batches, transferring it to a plate as it is ready. In the same pan, soften the onions over a gentle heat, then add the ginger, garlic and chilli. Fry for a few minutes before stirring in the spices – you will now have a nice spicy base for the curry. Add some seasoning and return all your meat to the pan, along with tinned tomatoes and the tomato purée. Simmer, partially covered, for about 10 minutes. Add the roughly chopped tomatoes and gently cook for a further 20 minutes.

Next, stir the spinach into the curry and allow it to wilt. Finally, add the coriander and taste to check the seasoning. Top each serving with a big dollop of soured cream and a sprinkle of garam masala.

quick CHAPATTIS

If you haven't got one (and why would you?), an empty wine bottle makes a good substitute for a rolling pin.

◀ MAKES 6

1 MUG (ABOUT 150G) WHOLEMEAL FLOUR
PINCH OF SALT
VEGETABLE OIL
100MLS WATER

Tip the flour into a big mixing bowl and add a pinch of salt. Mix water into the flour, a little at a time until you have a dryish dough, you will need about 100mls. Bring the dough together into a ball, then gently knead it on a lightly floured surface. Return the dough to the bowl, cover and leave to stand for 15-30 minutes.

Divide the dough into six golf ball sized pieces. Roll each ball out, until it is about the size of a small saucer, a couple of millimetres thick; use a little flour if the mixture is sticky.

Heat a frying pan or skillet over a hot flame with a dash of oil. Fry the chapattis for a minute on each side. Eat hot.

duck breasts with ginger and ORANGE, AND CELERIAC MASH

You can buy duck from the butcher at any time of year. That said it is well suited to winter cooking, especially with a bit of added warmth from orange, red wine and ginger.

◀ FOR 2
VEGETABLE OIL
2 PLUMP SKIN-ON DUCK BREASTS
CRUSHED SEA SALT AND PEPPER
HALF A GLASS RED WINE
3 CM PIECE OF ROOT GINGER, GRATED
JUICE AND ZEST OF A SMALL ORANGE

FOR THE CELERIAC MASH
1 CELERIAC ROOT (ABOUT 600G)
2 TBSP BUTTER
1 TBSP CRÈME FRAICHE
1 TBSP CHOPPED PARSLEY

Peel and chop the celeriac before boiling it in salted water for 10 minutes or until tender.

Meanwhile, heat a glug of oil in a frying pan over a medium hot flame. Score the skin of the duck breasts with a very sharp knife and season well with crushed sea salt and pepper. When the oil is hot, place the duck breasts skin side down in the pan and cook until the skin is golden and crispy, this will take 7-8 minutes if the breasts are really plump. Turn the duck breasts over and cook for a further 3-5 minutes until cooked to your liking (I prefer them pink in the middle).

When the celeriac is ready, drain it and mash with the butter, crème fraiche and parsley – it won't be smooth like potato mash but it will be rich and creamy. Season well.

Once you are happy with the duck, remove it from the pan and let it rest on a plate for a few minutes. Drain all but a tablespoon of fat from the pan, then return the pan to the heat and pour in the wine. Bubble for a few moments before adding the ginger, orange juice and zest. Bubble for a further minute or so. In posh circles they'd call this deglazing but I say it's all about using the juicy bits from the duck to create a yummy sauce.

Slice the duck breasts, serve on top of the celeriac mash and drizzle with the sauce.

welsh rarebit with REAL ALE

Eat as is or topped with crispy bacon. Either way, have a glass of good Welsh ale (Gwaun Valley is cracking if you can get it) at your side and the bottle of Worcestershire sauce should you wish to add a drizzle or two as you eat.

FOR 4

2 TBSP PLAIN FLOUR

2 TBSP SOFT BUTTER

150MLS MILK

3 TBSP DARK ALE

6 GENEROUS TBSP GRATED MATURE ENGLISH CHEDDAR

2 TSP ENGLISH MUSTARD

1 TSP WORCESTERSHIRE SAUCE

1 LARGE EGG

4 LARGE SLICES SOURDOUGH OR OTHER RUSTIC BREAD

First put the flour, butter and milk into a pan, heat together, whisking continuously, until you have a thick smooth sauce.

Take the pan off the heat and whisk in the ale – little by little. Mix in the cheese, mustard, Worcestershire sauce, egg and a pinch of salt. Toast the bread lightly, under the grill, on both sides.

Thickly spread the rarebit mixture onto one side of each toasted slice, then grill for 4-5 minutes or until golden and bubbling.

sausages with white bean, GARLIC AND SAGE MASH

Camping requires some constants. And those are sausages and beans. But, of course, I never said how you had to have them. Try this and you'll never look back.

FOR 2-3
4 TBSP OLIVE OIL
2 CLOVES GARLIC, FINELY SLICED
6-8 PORK SAUSAGES
2 X 420G CANS BUTTER BEANS, DRAINED
3 TBSP CRÈME FRAICHE OR CREAM
SMALL KNOB OF BUTTER
HANDFUL SMALL SAGE LEAVES

Heat the oil and garlic in a smallish pan, gently cook for 6-7 minutes or until the garlic is lightly golden and the oil infused. Meanwhile fry the sausages for 10-12 minutes.

When the sausages are nearly cooked, mix the beans into the garlic oil, then mash them together with some seasoning. Stir in the crème fraiche and taste – beans need lots of seasoning.

Transfer the sausages to plates. Wipe out the sausage pan. Heat the butter in the pan and when foaming, fry the sage till crispy with a sprinkling of sea salt.

Pile the bean mash and sausages onto plates, scatter with the crispy sage.

cheat's nutmeggy
RICE PUD WITH JAM

Whilst I'm not one to encourage convenience, there are occasions when only the very best will do. And that, my camping chums, is Devon creamed rice. You know it. To make this extra special, soak some juicy pitted prunes in a couple of tablespoons of Armagnac and eat with the creamy rice instead of jam. Or, tip the hot mixture into two shallow dishes, sprinkle with soft brown sugar and grill till burnished in places, eat with tart poached fruit.

FOR 2
425G TIN DEVON CREAMED RICE
2 TBSP DOUBLE OR WHIPPING CREAM OR 1 TBSP CLOTTED CREAM
WHOLE NUTMEG, FOR GRATING
2 STRIPS OF LEMON PEEL
YOUR FAVOURITE JAM (BLACKCURRANT OR RASPBERRY ARE PARTICULARLY NICE)

Empty the tin of rice into a pan and stir in the cream. Grate in a quarter of a whole nutmeg, add the strips of lemon peel and mix together. Gently heat the rice over a low heat and when piping hot, tip into bowls. Top with a spoonful of jam.

15 MINUTE chocolatey pud

FOR 2

SOFT UNSALTED BUTTER
2 SLICES BRIOCHE
2-3 TSP CASTER SUGAR
2 TBSP FLAKED ALMONDS
1 LARGE PEAR, PEELED AND SLICED INTO 8
1 TBSP HAZELNUT CHOCOLATE SPREAD
100MLS WHIPPING CREAM

Preheat the grill. Lightly butter one side of each slice of brioche and put the slices into the grill pan. Sprinkle the buttered sides evenly with a thin layer of sugar, followed by the flaked almonds.

Heat a small knob of butter in a frying pan and fry the slices of pear for 2-3 minutes until softened and golden. Transfer to a plate, cover to keep warm.

When the pan has cooled slightly, add the hazelnut chocolate spread, the cream and a small pinch of salt to the pan and gently stir together over a low heat. Meanwhile, grill the slices of brioche until the edges and the nuts are golden brown.

Transfer the brioche slices to plates, top with the pear slices and spoon the sauce on top. Eat as soon as possible.

cocktail for winter – SPICED PERRY

Perry has recently come back into vogue which is wonderful as it is the most delicious cidery pear drink. Warming after a Christmas dip or just warming. It's up to you.

FOR 6
4 MUGFULS (ABOUT 1 LITRE) PERRY
4 TBSP CALVADOS (APPLE BRANDY), OPTIONAL
JUICE OF A LARGE LEMON
CINNAMON STICK
VANILLA POD, HALVED
WHOLE NUTMEG, FOR GRATING
5 OR 6 CLOVES
2 SMALL PEARS, CORED AND SLICED
2 TBSP RUNNY HONEY, PLUS EXTRA IF NEEDED

Put everything into a pan together and simmer gently over a low heat for 10-15 minutes, giving the perry a stir now and then, tasting, and adding more honey if needed.
Strain the liquid through a sieve and into a jug. Discard the cinnamon stick, vanilla pod and cloves, then divide the slices of mulled pear between the mugs followed by the spiced brew.

A TEA FOR THE WINTER: Lemon Balm tea
Lemon Balm tea is well known to raise the spirits. A medicinal herb, the fresh leaves emit a lemony aroma when rubbed between the fingers, releasing an essential oil commonly known as citronella (so growing or drinking this in the summer could help keep those pesky midges at bay). Also known as the 'gentle balm', it is the perfect antidote to those dark winter nights.

MAKING THE PERFECT CUPPA
Use 1-2 teaspoons of leaves per cup. Place the lot in a teapot and add boiling water. Steep for 10 minutes. Keep the pot covered, in order to stop the essential oils from escaping.

The Christmas Day charity swim

If you've never taken part in a Christmas Day charity swim then you simply must. In fact, so must I. People assure me that the act of running into the sea in the company of a bunch of other crazy people in fancy dress for a good cause is a very exhilarating thing to do indeed. I applaud them. But not enough to actually take part.

In December the average sea surface temperature will have dropped significantly from the mildly Baltic summer temperatures, but they won't have reached the coldest of the year. So let's face facts. If you're in the south, you'll be looking at dashing into seas that are around 10°C. But if you're on the east coast, Newcastle for example, it's going to be more like eight degrees. That's without taking into account the wind chill. Brrrrr. And January and February can see the sea temperature drop as low as 5 or 6°C. Now that ain't funny.

HERE'S HOW IT WORKS:

* You tell your friends that you're going to take a dip in the sea for your favourite charity.
* Your friends laugh and say, 'You'll never do it, you pussy.'
* You reply with, 'Yes I will and, if I do, will you give me cash for my favourite charity?' Not wishing to appear mean, they say yes.
* You stay true to your word and take a dip.
* Your friends pay up and your charity continues its good work.

Getting into the water

Take the plunge! Much of the acclimatisation process is mental – knowing the moment of immersion will feel cold and embracing it anyway.

Exhale as you jump in. In cold water the rib cage contracts, which leads many swimmers to feeling they can't breathe. Exhale and the next breath will come naturally in. Shrieking, grunting and fwaw-fwaw-fwawing for your first strokes are perfectly natural accompaniments to a wild swim.

Wait 90 seconds. The pleasure of open water might not be immediate. Give your body a little time to react and your circulation will soon start charging around and you'll feel alive. Swimming outdoors is medically proven to be good for circulation.

But then, let's not forget the dangers...

The main safety risk you face as a wild swimmer is getting too cold. As your body loses heat your blood shunts to the core to keep organs warm; your muscles slow, arms and legs become weak and swimming becomes increasingly difficult. So, even if you are doing a dash and a dip, stay close to the shore.

Other risks of jumping into cold water include: cold shock, hypothermia, cramp, heart attack, asthma and cold water hives.

So, if you have a heart condition or asthma then you are excused. Of course if you decide not to take part you must go and watch. Or better still persuade your friends to take part and then watch, although this carries a risk in itself.

When you get out, I suggest you get wrapped up warm asap. Get dressed as soon as you can, out of the wind. Don't let your tootsies get a chill, so put on socks and shoes as quickly as possible and put on as many layers as you have. Once you have dried off, you can celebrate your charitable deeds with a sip of spiced perry (see page 281).

Where to take part in a charity swim

I suspect some of these will be colder than others and no doubt there will be somewhere near you that I've left out. But as long as I've sowed the seeds then the rest is up to you. And if you can't swim, take plenty of cash to chuck into the charity buckets.

CHRISTMAS DAY
Boscombe Pier, Bournemouth
Porthcawl, Bridgend
Bude, Falmouth, Portreath, Sennen Cove and
   Trevaunance Cove (St Agnes), Cornwall
Exmouth, Devon
Charmouth and Weymouth, Dorset
Brighton, East Sussex
Cromer and Hunstanton, Norfolk
Aldeburgh, Felixstowe and Lowestoft, Suffolk

NEW YEAR'S DAY
Lyme Regis, Dorset
Peel, Isle of Man
Abersoch, Llyn Peninsula
Saundersfoot, Pembrokeshire

BOXING DAY
Aberdeen, Aberdeenshire
Charlestown, Cornwall
Bridport, Dorset
Liverpool Albert Dock, Lancashire
Abersoch, Llyn Peninsula
Burghead, Moray
Whitley Bay, North Tyneside
Tenby, Pembrokeshire
Prestwick, South Ayrshire
Seaburn, Sunderland

Christmas in the camper

Now then. I'm not going to pretend that I've ever spent Christmas Day in a camper because I haven't. Sadly, I am usually tied to the kitchen. It's where you'll find me early on Christmas morning, prepping the turkey so that I can sneak out for my Christmas Day surf once the kids have opened their presents. After that, it's a couple of pints at the Coach and Horses before donning the comedy apron for a little half-cut gravy making. To be honest, it's not a bad scene.

There are years when I'd rather be away from the telly and the traditions. Sometimes I think it would be better all round if we made our excuses and left, just for a couple of days, if only we could. At times like these, the thought of Christmas dinner in the van, far away from civilisation, looks like a very clever strategy indeed. You wouldn't even have to give up the essential Yuletide trappings. A little tinsel goes a long way in a camper van. Singing, of course, would still be allowed.

Don't get me wrong because I love Christmas as much as the next man, but come Christmas afternoon it wouldn't be unusual to catch me looking out of the kitchen window at the van with a winsome look on my face. That look would tell a thousand words if it were a picture, which I am sure it isn't. On seeing it you'd excuse me from the washing-up with the dangle of a set of keys, a Thermos of hot soup and a little pressie to open when I got there. Honestly, I can be unbearable sometimes.

If you are one of the masses of van-owning, unencumbered, footloose and fancy-free souls who can take off whenever you like, then this is for you.

Happy Christmas!

Menu

{Happy Chistmas}

- Smoked Salmon with pickled cucumber
- Turkey with sage stuffing crumbs
- Root veggies with chestnuts + parsley
- Essential buttery Sprouts
- Cranberry clementine compote
- Mulled pears
- Pistachio and chocolate Pamettone chistmascake

Christmas countdown

10am
First thing with a cuppa in hand...
Make the cranberry compote, spoon into a bowl
Make the mulled pears, transfer to a bowl
Fry the stuffing 'crumbs', tip onto a plate
Steam the root veggies, tip into a bowl
Pickle the cucumber
Trim and peel the sprouts

12.30pm
Finish the starter and devour with a glass of fizz.

1pm
Bring a pan of salted water to the boil for the sprouts.

1.15pm
Fry the turkey, boil the sprouts.
Drain the sprouts, tip back into the pan with seasoning
and butter and shake over the heat, then tip into a bowl
(warm it under the grill first if you can) and cover to keep
warm. Tip the root veggies into the pan – reheat with the
chestnuts, parsley and olive oil.

1.30pm
Serve your main course feast. Warm and tuck into the
mulled pears when you fancy.

smoked salmon with
PICKLED CUCUMBER

Right then. Christmas day is never an easy affair, but if you're in the van you're going to need to be extra prepared. This starter requires nothing more than some chopping, a bowl and a few bits and pieces. Couldn't be easier. Honest.

FOR 2
HALF A CUCUMBER
JUICE OF A LARGE LIME
2 TSP CASTER SUGAR
HALF A RED CHILLI, DESEEDED AND FINELY CHOPPED
250G SMOKED SALMON, SLICED
4 TBSP GREEK YOGHURT
SODA OR SOURDOUGH BREAD, TO SERVE

Peel and thinly slice the cucumber. Mix the lime juice, caster sugar and red chilli together in a shallow bowl. Add the cucumber slices and turn in the mixture – set aside for 30 minutes (or a few hours), giving it another turn now and then. Pile the cucumber onto a plate with the salmon and a small bowl of yoghurt. Tuck in with some bread on the side.

turkey with 'SAGE STUFFING' CRUMBS

Quick and easy to cook, escalopes replace the usual bird, and the stuffing with sage and lemon is cooked till golden and sprinkled over the turkey at the last minute.

FOR 4
50G READY-MADE DRIED OR HOMEMADE WHITE BREADCRUMBS
2 TBSP FINELY CHOPPED SAGE (OR GOOD PINCH OF DRIED)
BUTTER AND OIL, FOR FRYING
ZEST OF A LEMON AND JUICE OF 2
PLAIN FLOUR, FOR DUSTING
8-10 PIECES FREE RANGE TURKEY BREAST ESCALOPE (ABOUT 575G)

In a bowl, mix the breadcrumbs with the sage and some salt and pepper. Heat a knob of butter in a frying pan and fry the crumbs for 4-5 minutes, till golden, stirring. Stir the lemon zest into the crumbs, then tip them onto a plate to cool.

Mix a little flour with some seasoning and dust the turkey escalopes on both sides.

Wipe out the frying pan, then heat another knob of butter and a slug of oil in it. Once sizzling, fry the turkey escalopes, in batches, for 2-3 minutes on each side or until tinged brown and cooked through. Transfer to a platter, as they are ready, and cover with foil to keep warm.

Add the lemon juice to the pan and bubble over the heat, stir in a tiny knob of butter, whisk together and drizzle over the cooked turkey, then scatter with the crumbs.

root veggies with
CHESTNUTS AND PARSLEY

2 MEDIUM PARSNIPS

4 MEDIUM CARROTS

4 SMALLISH POTATOES, SCRUBBED

OLIVE OIL

200G COOKED PEELED CHESTNUTS

2-3 TBSP CHOPPED PARSLEY

Peel the parsnips and carrots and scrub the potatoes. Cut all the vegetables into roughly 3 cm chunks. Bring a pan of water to the boil and put a steamer on top of the pan. Steam all the vegetables for 15-20 minutes or until tender. Drain the pan and tip the vegetables into it with a glug of olive oil, the chestnuts, parsley and some seasoning. Toss together over the heat for a few minutes.

ESSENTIAL buttery sprouts

4 HANDFULS BRUSSELS SPROUTS, TRIMMED AND PEELED

A KNOB OF BUTTER

Bring a pan of salted water to the boil. Simmer the sprouts for 3-4 minutes or until tender – overcook them at your peril. Drain the sprouts, tip them back into the pan, add the butter and some seasoning and swirl together.

cranberry clementine COMPOTE

150G CRANBERRIES

ZEST AND JUICE OF 2 CLEMENTINES

50G CASTER OR LIGHT SOFT BROWN SUGAR

1 CINNAMON STICK

Put all the ingredients in a pan and simmer over a low-medium heat for 20-25 minutes or until the fruit has collapsed and cooked, giving it a stir now and then. Leave to cool.

mulled honey pears

Another one pan wonder. This is simple and delicious and needs just one pan plus a few other bits and pieces. Heck, give the washing-up fairy the day off and eat it straight from the dish. Who could wait anyway? It looks delicious. Trust me, it is.

FOR 4
200MLS RED WINE
2 TBSP HONEY
JUICE OF AN ORANGE AND A FEW PIECES OF PEEL
1 MULLED WINE SPICE SACHET
4 RIPE BUT FIRM PEARS
MASCARPONE MIXED WITH A LITTLE EXTRA HONEY, TO SERVE

Pour the wine into a pan. Add the honey, the orange juice and peel and the mulled wine sachet. Stir together and bring the liquid to simmering point, stirring. Peel the pears, leaving the stalks intact.

Add the pears to the liquid, bring the liquid back to a simmer and cover the pan. Poach the pears for 15-20 minutes, turning them from time to time in the liquid so they colour evenly.

Take the pears out of the liquid and set aside. Bubble the liquid in the pan, with the lid on, until syrupy, 7-8 minutes. Spoon the syrup over the pears and leave to cool. Eat with a spoonful of honeyed mascarpone.

Pistachio and chocolate
PANETTONE CHRISTMAS CAKES

Who says you need to miss out on Christmas cake? No one. Just because you can't bake doesn't mean you can't enjoy a slice with the re-runs of *The Wizard of Oz*. Oh. Hang on, there is no *Wizard of Oz* this year. Time for a celebration.

Add a couple of mini sparklers to each and light as you present them (obviously it won't be a surprise but, you know, it's fun). If you can't find sugar-nibbed panettone, add a sprinkle of icing sugar too.

FOR 4

2 MINI SUGAR-NIBBED PANETTONE
4 TBSP MASCARPONE
2 TSP ICING SUGAR
3 TBSP CHOPPED PISTACHIOS
50G DARK CHOCOLATE, CHOPPED

Remove each panettone from its paper liner. Slice each one into three horizontally. Mix together the mascarpone, icing sugar, pistachios and a third of the chocolate.

Spread a layer of the mascarpone mixture over the cut side of the base of each panettone, then top with the middle layer. Spread a second layer of the mascarpone mix and then put the tops onto each cake.

Melt the remaining chocolate and drizzle over the top of each panettone for a snow-capped effect. Leave to dry before tucking in.

south west dubs
SWD
vw panzers

Places to stay

I love camping and I love campsites, but I'm not a big fan of the packaged up and laid out, the overcrowded and the mass market. There is a time and a place for these, like at VW festivals and special weekends away when the kids can spend all day in the pool and me and the missus can get a few zeds in the sunshine without worrying. But give me a quiet camping spot overlooking a beach with a few nice neighbours and a decent pub within easy walk and I am happy.

Are you with me? If you are, then you seriously need to heed the bit of advice that's coming up ANY MINUTE NOW.

THE CAMPING AND CARAVAN CLUB

www.campingandcaravanningclub.co.uk

The 'Friendly Club' has more than 1,400 certificated sites all over the UK. These are privately run, member-only sites that allow up to five campervans, caravan and motorhomes and up to ten tents. That means you can (almost) guarantee a quiet time with just you and the countryside for company. Certificated sites are categorised by their style and offer hideaways in remote areas, family sites with activities and facilities for kids, sites with leisure activities such as fishing or swimming and sites with accommodation for non-campers. There are also certificated sites attached to pubs and adults-only sites.

BRITSTOPS

www.britstops.com

In 2011 a new membership scheme began, based on the highly successful 'France Passion' scheme. In exchange for a membership fee (£25), motorhomers and camper vanners can now stop overnight, for free, as a guest at participating farms, vineyards, farm shops, local breweries and even a Scottish smokehouse. The scheme puts authentic, local produce together with camper vans in the very best way.

Britstops are a great way to make more of the countryside. However, your hosts are obliged to offer nothing more than a level pitch for you to park for 24 hours, so you'll need to be self-contained. There is no guarantee you'll be able to have a shower or use their loo. But if you've got a Porta Potti on board and don't mind going without a wash for a day or so, I say go for it.

CAMPING IN THE ROUGH

For me, the point of owning a camper van is being able to wake up within sight of the sea. This can be a problem in many places unless you stay on a campsite because of local by-laws banning overnight parking and camping at beachside car parks.

After all, wild camping is technically illegal in England, Wales and Northern Ireland. It is a civil offence, which means that you can only be made to move with the help of a court order. It's also worth mentioning here that camping on the Queen's highway will more than likely gain the attention of the boys in blue very quickly so it's one to avoid unless you are absolutely knackered and have no choice but to stop in a lay-by.

TOLERATED SPOTS There are some places where wild camping is tolerated. This means that the owners or operators are willing to turn a blind eye to anyone who wants to park up for the night. These spots are very precious and anyone using them should feel privileged to be able to. Forums such as www.wildcamping.co.uk are good places to start looking.

Local councils also have the power to allow camper vans and motorhomes to use their car parks for overnight stopovers. Not enough of them do. However, there are a few places around the UK where you can wake up to the sound of the waves in return for a small fee. Some are listed here: www.ukmotorhomes.net/uk-motorhome-stopovers.shtml.

WILD RULES Thinking about wild camping? Then here are a few things to think about before you set off:

★ Don't just leave it as you found it, leave it better than you found it.
★ If you get asked to move on, do it with good grace and a sense of humour.
★ If you can, check with the locals that it's OK before you park up.
★ Be respectful and don't be a nuisance or play loud music, especially early or late.

STAYING AT THE PUB

One of the drawbacks of camping in winter is losing the light so early and having nothing to do except cosy up in the van and play cards, watch a DVD or read a book. Now that's all very nice if you have great heating. But after a few days it can start to get a little wearing, not to mention cold.

The solution of course? The pub! There are plenty of publicans who won't mind you staying in their car parks as long as you treat the place with respect and don't expect to settle in for the week. In fact, it can sometimes be a win–win situation for both of you because you get a nice warm fire to sit next to and the publican gets you to chuck a few quid behind the bar.

THE MOTORHOME STOPOVER CLUB
www.motorhomestopover.co.uk
This is a members' scheme that has over 500 pubs listed as places to stop the night for free. It's £30 to join but with an average night on a campsite costing about the same, who's to say it isn't great value? Phone ahead to check that they are OK with you pitching up and putting your head down – on the understanding that you'll at least spend a few quid in the bar.

PUBS WITH CAMPSITES
www.pubcampsites.com and www.pubcamping.co.uk
There are plenty of great pubs with great campsites, although you should probably expect to pay for the privilege. More than likely these kinds of places will have more facilities than your run-of-the-mill car park so expect to be able to clean your teeth and have a shower without raising an eyebrow.

DO IT THE 'JUST ASK' WAY Sometimes you don't want to plan ahead do you? The only drawback is getting to five o'clock and finding that you have nowhere sorted. The easy way to get around this is to ask very politely if the landlord minds if you pitch up in return for buying a meal or a few drinks. Home-made steak and ale pie and a pint of Old Peculiar? I'm in. Please note that this only works if everyone behaves courteously (and that includes the landlord).

THE SMALL PRINT Be aware that the rozzers might not like you having a skinful and then sleeping in your van, in the same way they don't like people kipping in their cars in public places after a night out. Spare a thought for your licence. That is all.

CAMPER VAN HIRE COMPANIES, UK AND IRELAND (AND A COUPLE IN EUROPE)

SOUTH EAST

Norfolk VW Campers
Mulbarton, Norfolk
07875 404747
www.norfolkvwcampers.co.uk

East Coast Campers
Canvey Island, Essex
01268 515446
www.eastcoastcampers.co.uk

Ilovevdubadventures
Lincoln
01522 543659 or 07852 255638
www.ilovevdubadventures.co.uk

Camp in a VDub
Woking, Surrey
08712 344331
www.campinavdub.co.uk

Hippy Campers
London
07538 484180
www.hippycampers.com

SOUTH

Isle of Wight Camper Van Holidays
Shanklin, Isle of Wight
01983 852089 or 07855 431566
www.isleofwightcampers.co.uk

Campervan Rental
Wareham, Dorset
01929 553336
www.vwcampervanrental.co.uk

Vanillas Splits Ltd
Barnham, West Sussex
01243 545725
www.vanillasplits.com

Brighton Rock Campers
Brighton, Sussex
07970 881346
www.brightonrockcampers.com

Campervanatics
Hove, Sussex
01273 241820
www.campervanatics.co.uk

SOUTH WEST

O'Connors Campers
Okehampton, Devon
01837 659599
www.oconnorscampers.co.uk

Classic Campervan Hire
Tavistock, Devon
08009709147 or 01822617220
www.classiccampervanhire.co.uk

Devon Classic Campers
South Molton, Devon
07774 725083
www.devonclassiccampers.co.uk

Comfy Campers
Cheltenham, Gloucestershire
01242 696774
www.comfycampers.co.uk

South West Camper Hire
Exeter, Devon
01392 811931
www.southwestcamperhire.com

BaseCampers Campervan Hire
Padstow, Cornwall
07821 155786
www.basecampers.net

MIDLANDS

Camper 4 Hire
Coalville, Leicestershire
07747 771150
www.camper4hire.co.uk

Outer Motive
Warwick
01926 743107 or 01926 408942
www.outermotive.co.uk

Shropshire Camper Hire
Shrewsbury, Shropshire
01743 361229
www.shropshirecamperhire.co.uk

NORTH

BumbleVee Campers
Doncaster, South Yorkshire
07585 608774 or 07585 608744
www.bumblevee.co.uk

Liberty Campers
Otley, West Yorkshire
07904 190830
www.libertycampers.co.uk

Lakeland Campers
Kendal, Cumbria
01539 824357
www.lakelandcampers.co.uk

Chase the Sun Ltd
Preston
01772 716694 or 07979 863491
www.chasethesun.co.uk

Generation Campers
Sheffield
07963 155195
www.generationcampers.co.uk

Camperscape Ltd
Tynemouth, Tyne & Wear
07813 176099
www.camperscape.co.uk

Jolly Campervans
Huddersfield, Yorkshire
07715 000375
www.jollycampervans.co.uk

Lakes Camper Hire
Ulverston, Cumbria
01539 530763 or 07717 116562
www.lakescamperhire.co.uk

WALES

Vintage VW Weddings
South Glamorgan, Wales
07817 226550
www.vintagevwweddings.co.uk

SCOTLAND

Out There Campers
Nairn, Inverness
07912 138727
www.outtherecampers.co.uk

**South West Scotland Classic
VW Campers**
Carrutherstown, Dumfries
07789 681739
www.solwaybeetles.co.uk

Happy Highland Campers
Dingwall, Scotland
01349 830214
www.happyhighlandcampers.
co.uk

Highland Campervans
Dalcross, Inverness
01667 493976
www.highlandcampervans.com

Daisy Campers
Dollar, Scotland
01259 743800
www.daisycampers.co.uk

IRELAND

Detour Campervans
Navan/Dublin Airport
+353 (0)469031481
www.detour.ie

Lazydays
Wicklow, Ireland
+353 (0)872885771
www.lazydays.ie

Tourtoise Tours
Co Antrim, Northern Ireland
07809 626358
www.tourtoisetours.com

EUROPE

Fiesta Campervans
Asturias, Spain
00 34 674219528
www.fiestacampervans.co.uk

Belle Vie Holiday Adventures
Atlantic coast, Landes, SW
France
+447810633444
www.holidaycampers.fr

Camper Experience
Montfoort, Holland
0031-302232957
www.camperexperience.nl

The camper van year

MARCH
Brighton Vegan Fayre: Music, cookery and bars at www.brighton.vegfest.co.uk
Falmouth Spring Flower Show: A bloomin' great event. www.falmouthshow.co.uk
Goth Festival, Whitby: Bram Stoker-inspired stalls, music, mayhem and a lot of dressing up. www.whitbygothweekend.co.uk
Swanage Blues Festival: Traditional blues on the Dorset coast. www.swanage-blues.org

APRIL
Brighton Food Festival: Food, beer, fun for ten days. www.brightonfoodfestival.com
Chocolate Festival, Brighton: I will say no more. www.festivalchocolate.co.uk
National Motorhome Show, Peterborough: Go along and see what you could have won! www.outandaboutlive.co.uk
Scarborough Literature Festival: Top line-up. www.scarboroughliteraturefestival.co.uk
The Big Bournemouth Beer Festival: All the Bs and all the beers here on the sunny south coast. www.bic.co.uk

MAY
Cathedral Quarter Arts Festival, Belfast: Arts and family entertainment with an Irish slant. www.cqaf.com
International Donkey week, Devon: www.donkeysanctuary.org.uk
Rochester Sweeps Festival, Kent: The biggest gathering of Morris Men in the world. How can you resist? www.whatsonmedway.co.uk
Spirit of Speyside Whisky Festival: If you love whisky, this must surely be it. www.spiritofspeyside.co.uk
Weymouth International Kites Festival: Wowser! Kite flyers from all over the world. Fireworks too. Much fun and a sore neck by the end of it. www.visitweymouth.co.uk

JUNE

Eden Sessions, Cornwall: An otherworldly night out under the stars. Great line-ups too. www.edensessions.co.uk

Goldcoast Oceanfest, North Devon: Surf, girls, surf, boys, surf, fun, surf, music, surf, sport. And all with an eco heart. Love it. www.goldcoastoceanfest.co.uk

North Devon Festival: Thirty days' celebration on the glorious North Devon coast. www.northdevontheatres.org.uk/north_devon_festival.asp

Nudefest, Cornwall: All kinds of nudie activities including yoga, music, dancing, body painting and sports. You'll be very welcome. www.nudefest.co.uk

South Wales Boat Show, Swansea: They say that boat ownership is like tearing up £50 notes in the shower. A bit like owning a camper then, only wetter. Go and see for yourself. www.southwalesboatshow.co.uk/

World Naked Bike Ride: Awareness event to protest at oil-dependent culture. Alternatively, the world worm-charming championships take place the same week. www.worldnakedbikeride.org

JULY

Brighton and Hove Pride Festival: One of the largest gay and lesbian festivals in the UK. www.brightonpride.org

British Beach Polo Championships, Dorset: Posh sport, posh neighbourhood. What's not to love? Not for the likes of me I'm afraid but you know, why not? www.sandpolo.com

Hebridean Celtic Festival: Fab location, great Celtic music and very far away from it all. Take me there now! www.hebceltfest.com

King's Lynn Festival Too, Norfolk: One of Europe's biggest free music festivals. Street performers and acts such as The Wanted. You know you want it. www.festivaltoo.co.uk

Maritime Weekend, Hull Marina: Go for the sea shanties – and much more… www.visithullandeastyorkshire.com

Paddle round the pier, Brighton: The UK's biggest FREE watersports event. Music and festivities too. And all FREE. www.paddleroundthepier.com

Really Wild Food Festival, St Davids: Wild food, foraging and general all-round goodness in the Pembrokeshire National Park. www.reallywildfestival.co.uk

Sproai Festival, Waterford: Big festival vibe organised by local Irish street theatre group. www.spraoi.com

The Great British Skinny Dip: One big day of baring all. If you've never done a skinny dip, this is the time to try. www.greatbritishskinnydip.info

UK National Sandcastle Competition, Woolacombe Beach, North Devon: www.northdevonhospice.org.uk/event/all-events/uk-national-sandcastle-competition.ashx

Wakestock, Aberoch: Wakeboarding and other coolness abound at this hyper-hip music and water festival. Extreme. www.wakestock.co.uk

Whitstable Oyster Festival, Kent: Oysters aren't the only thing on the menu. www.whitstableoysterfestival.com

AUGUST

Bournemouth Air Festival. More neck craning stuff on the south coast. www.bournemouthair.co.uk

Dippers and Dunkers Festival, Margate: A fantastical celebration of everything from burlesque to magic, circus to seaside entertainment. Proper seaside stuff. www.dippersanddunkers.org.uk

Garlic Festival, Isle of Wight: Music and garlic combine in a heady mix. Chart-topping acts have included The Wurzels and Alvin Stardust. Glasto it is not, but worth a trundle. www.garlic-festival.co.uk

National Kissing Day: Get involved but don't tell the wife. www.kissingday.co.uk

Portsmouth Kite Festival: Another look to the skies, with strings attached. www.portsmouthkitefestival.org.uk

The British Fireworks Championships Finals, Plymouth: Oooooh. Aaaaaah. Lots of bangs, whizzes and whistles. www.britishfireworks.co.uk

Weymouth Carnival, Dorset: Red Arrows and everything! With 100,000 people going, parking might be sticky on the seafront that week. www.weymouthcarnival.co.uk

SEPTEMBER

Agatha Christie Festival, Torbay: Treasure Hunts, teas, murder mystery games and even a swim (?). The plot thickens. www.englishriviera.co.uk/agathachristie/festival

Beachwatch Big Weekend: Marine Conservation Society's annual clean-up. Every piece of marine litter is recorded in a bid to influence legislation. Get involved and make a difference. www.mcsuk.org

Bridport Hat Festival, Dorset: Expect fascinators, boonies, beanies and bonnets and maybe even the odd stovepipe. Be prepared to doff it for the ladies. www.bridporthatfest.org

Coastal Currents Festival, Hastings: Art in a beach hut? Count me in. www.coastalcurrents.org.uk

Galway Oyster Festival, Galway: Guinness, craic and the world oyster-opening championships. I'm there already. www.galwaysoysterfest.com

Switching on the lights, Blackpool: Our number one, fave attraction. www.blackpool-illuminations.net

The World Bellyboarding Championships, Cornwall: Good, old-fashioned day out on the beach with comps and prizes. www.bellyboarding.co.uk

Windfest: Wind and watersports on Poole's gorgeous sands. www.animalwindfest.co.uk

World Fireworks Championships, Blackpool: The world's best gather to out-sparkle each other on the prom. Not one for the family pet. www.visitblackpool.com

World Stone Skimming Championships, Argyle: A disused quarry gives the water the perfect surface for a splish splash plop ... www.stoneskimming.com

OCTOBER

Eastbourne Beer Festival: One hundred and twenty cask ales and beers are sure to bring the town to life. www.eastbournebeerfestival.co.uk

Kent's Coastal Week: Events and wildlife galore, every October half term. www.kent.gov.uk/coastalweek

Swanage Blues Festival: A hootenanny by the sea. Yeehar. www.swanage-blues.org

NOVEMBER

Blackpool Christmas Lights Switch-On: Hot on the heels of the illuminations comes the Christmas switch-on. Watts and watts of power light up the promenade. www.visitblackpool.com

Clovelly Herring Festival, North Devon: Bideford Bay was once home to a fleet of herring boats that would take to the water every autumn in search of the 'silver darlings of the sea'. This keeps the tradition alive with sea shanties and other herring-related business. www.clovelly.co.uk

Movember: Not strictly coastal but worth a mention. Shave on the 20th October then grow the biggest 'tache you can by the end of the month. I did it but mine was rubbish. www.movember.com

DECEMBER

International Tea Day: 15th December is the day we down tools and have a cuppa to think about those who provide us with the greatest drink of them all.

JANUARY

Bath Tub Race, Poole: Crazy antics to celebrate the New Year. I'd wear a wetsuit if I were you. www.poolelifeboat.co.uk

New Year's Day Dip: See events on page 284.

Up Helly Aa: Fire and ice festival in the Shetlands with much drinking and merriment. Concludes with a longship on fire. Cripes. www.uphellyaa.org

FEBRUARY

Coastival, Scarborough: A festival of music, dance, comedy, theatre and everything in between from the quintessential coastal town. www.coastival.com

National Sickie Day: First Monday in February is supposed to be the worst day for sickies the whole year. Go on, pull one.

Rye Bay Scallop Week, Kent: Cookery demonstrations, scallop races, the lot, all celebrating Rye's long association with the humble scallop. www.ryebayscallops. co.uk

Taking action: the war on plastic!

This book would not be complete without a little word about marine litter. Plastic is my thing you see. But if it isn't yours and you're one of those people who can't stand all these environmentalists going on about this and couldn't care less about the state of the coast, you might want to look away now.

OK. Now open your eyes. What do you see?

I see a shoreline that's littered with bits of plastic, plastic bags, the sticks of cotton buds, pieces of polystyrene and plastic bottles. I see my playground drowning in mess. I see 17,000 miles of coastline becoming choked with rubbish. Whilst I am a cheery kind of a chappie, I am at war with plastic in the ocean. Here's why:

Floating plastic can be mistaken for food by seabirds and fish.

Plastic in the marine environment changes. Firstly it breaks down into smaller and smaller pieces then it begins to degrade, leaching potentially toxic chemicals and having a devastating effect on the animals that come into contact with it.

If a fish eats a smaller fish that's eaten a smaller fish that's eaten a tiny piece of plastic, where does that leave us? Eating our own mess. We can't allow that to happen can we?

The Pacific Garbage Patch is growing. There is now a floating patch of plastic gathered in the North Pacific gyre that is estimated to be between 700,000 square kilometres and 150,000 square kilometres. Flipping heck.

If plastic doesn't end up in an oceanic garbage patch or inside a sea bird or ingested by a fish then it will end up polluting our beaches.

WHAT CAN WE DO ABOUT IT?

Pick up a bottle and take it home for recycling. Think of it as a little thanks to your beach.

Stop using so much plastic. Take your own Bags for Life to the shops. Go bag free. Phase as much plastic out of your life as you can. It isn't easy but then it all counts.

Surfers Against Sewage (www.sas.org.uk) and www.beachclean.net organise beach cleans. Or simply organise your own. All you need is a few friends and a few plastic sacks. There. Half an hour later, job done.

Join The Marine Conservation Society (www.mcsuk.org) and adopt your local beach.

with grateful thanks to:

Elizabeth Hallett for her editorial judgement and guidance.

Al, Anna, Bea, Jaime, Mandi and Zelda and everyone else at Saltyard Books for their timely reminders and, you know, making it happen.

Sarah for cooking up a storm as usual.

Craig, Georgia and the rest of the team for making it all look gorgeous.

Borra, Jan and Kate at DML for believing in me.

Lindsay Bradbury for taking a punt.

Will Daws and everyone at Plum for putting me on telly. Brilliant.

Nico Chapman for riding shotgun and taking some awesome pics.

Damian Horner for being the enigma that he is.

Andy Price for learning to sail with me.

Richard Knight for the best day surfing without a board.

Andrew Cotton for riding those monsters and living to tell the tale.

Martin Knight, our own Isambard, for use of the brain inside that stovepipe hat.

Jamie and Nicky at Copy Monkey for the taking care of the office.

Laura Fennimore at the RNLI for help with the best of the best.

Tim Lidstone-Scott for help with info on the Norfolk Coast Path.

Ross and Alice at TYF for taking me on an amazing coastal adventure: www.tyf.com.

Kate Rew and everyone at The Outdoor Swimming Society for their swimming advice: www.outdoorswimmingsociety.com.

Peter Robinson, from the Museum of British Surfing, for his bellyboarding knowledge: www.museumofbritishsurfing.org.uk.

Julia Horton Powdrill for her Cawl recipe: www.reallywildfestival.co.uk.

Sally Parkin for getting us into the noble sport of lying down: www. originalsurfboards.co.uk.

Alyson Murray at www.hotsmoked.co.uk for the smoking advice.

Dan Garnett for his fishy chitchat: www.clovellyfish.co.uk.

Fraser Christian for a great day among the seaweed: www.coastalsurvival.com.

Andrew Welch of British Naturism.

Alison Dando for diving information: www.bsac.com.

Nick Holden for putting on a fine event: www.bellyboarding.co.uk.

Howies for their help and advice about cool weather camping clobber.

Danny Groves at the Whale and Dolphin Conservation Society.

Steve and Catherine Bunn for the advice about winterising your camper: www.highlandcampervans.com.
Mark at Just Kampers: www.justkampers.co.uk.
Harriet Hall at Blacks for sleeping bag advice: www.blacks.co.uk.
Justin Garanovich of the European Coaster Club for his top coasters.
Steven Neale for his top ten watery campsites.
Ian Reach at Natural England for his advice on collecting seaweed.
Ian Marchant at SW Classic VWs for advice on keeping it pretty: www.southwestvws.co.uk.
Stargazer Tom Trubridge for the help with celestial happenings.
Ben, Carly, Sonny, Millie, Mart, Kath, Tom, Jack, Trevor, Judy and Shannon. Great camping companions. And Artie, for loving the vegetarian option so much that he came out too soon.
Annie, Eddie and Lola for being themselves.
Dave Lamacraft for his bird-spotting knowledge and photos.
Sam, Paul and Penny at O'Connor's Campers: www.oconnorscampers.co.uk
Puffin Dive Centre, Oban for taking me for a chilly Scottish dip: www.puffin.org.uk
And finally. Joanne, Maggie, Charlie and Bob for coming along for the ride (even though sometimes they didn't want to).

... and from Sarah a special thank you to:

Elizabeth for her never-failing encouragement.
Matthew for his unconditional enthusiasm for my creations (even after the umpteenth mackerel recipe) and for expert camper van driving.
www.libertycampers.co.uk for letting us disappear into the Dales and beyond with Dougal, our trusty camper van.

Index

Anchovy mayo 78

apples: Pork, scrumpy, apple and fennel pot roast 237

apricots: Poached greengages or apricots with lemon and lime cream 169

Asparagus, egg and baby leek salad with creamy dressing 82

aubergines: Aubergine and mushroom curry 233

Aubergine, pepper and halloumi kebabs with lemony houmous 128

Ratatouille 161

bacon: Celeriac, crispy bacon and parsley couscous risotto 229

Colcannon cakes with smoky bacon 70

Nettle soup with crispy bacon 59

bananas: Raspberry and banana traybake with cinnamon crumble topping 32

Rocky road bananas 130

basil: Barbecued fish parcels with lemon basil butter 126

Sea bass with a simple fresh tomato and basil sauce 139

beans: Mart's chorizo and bean stew 270

Massaman chicken curry with beans and cashews 236

One pan lamb with peas, broad beans and mint 165

Sausages with white bean, garlic and sage mash 278

beef: Campervan steak and chips 230

Easy-peasy burgers 118

Mart's meaty meatballs 92–3

beetroot: Winter veg crisps 267

black pudding: Poached eggs with black pudding and sea beet 57

Blackberry lime fizz 238

The breakfast burrito 225

broad beans: One pan lamb with peas, broad beans and mint 165

broccoli: Purple sprouting with two extras 78

brussels sprouts: Essential buttery sprouts 293

burgers: Easy-peasy burgers 118

burritos: The breakfast burrito 225

butter beans: Mart's chorizo and bean stew 270

Sausages with white bean, garlic and sage mash 278

cabbage: Chunky colcannon 69

capers: Mackerel with mustard caper butter 180

Sea bass with olives and capers 85

carrageen moss: Martin's sea moss 53

carrots: Carrot and feta patties 81

Root veggies with chestnuts and parsley 293

cashew nuts: Massaman chicken curry with beans and cashews 236

Cauliflower carbonara 79

cawl: Julia's veggie cawl 68

celeriac: Celeriac, crispy bacon and parsley couscous risotto 229

Duck breasts with ginger and orange with celeriac mash 275

Chamomile tea 238

chapattis 274

cheese: Aubergine, pepper and halloumi kebabs with lemony houmous 128

Carrot and feta patties 81

Cauliflower carbonara 79

Cheese fondue 202

French onion soup with cheesy croutes 228

Goat's cheese on toast with thyme and honey 77

Parmesan shortbreads 28

Welsh rarebit with real ale 276

chestnuts: roasting 261

Root veggies with chestnuts and parsley 293

chicken: Barbecued chicken with Lebanese style salad 120

Campervan paella 166–7

Family fajitas with a simple salsa 90–1

Joanne's Cally chicken with tarragon and lemon 164

Massaman chicken curry with beans and cashews 236

Three ways with chicken 129

chillies: Squid in minutes, with pepper, orange and chilli 124

Tomato, chilli and mustard man jam 119

chips: Campervan steak and chips 230

Fish and chips 141

chocolate: Chocolate hokey pokey bites 31

15 minute chocolatey pud 280

Pistachio and chocolate panettone Christmas cakes 296

Rocky road bananas 130

chorizo: The breakfast burrito 225

Campervan paella 166–7

Clams with chorizo and sherry 46
Mackerel with tomatoes, chorizo and fennel seed 180
Mart's chorizo and bean stew 270
cinnamon: Maple and cinnamon popcorn 203
    Raspberry and banana traybake with cinnamon
    crumble topping 32
Clams with chorizo and sherry 46
clementines: Cranberry clementine compote 293
colcannon: Chunky colcannon 69
    Colcannon cakes with smoky bacon 70
Corned beef hash 266
courgettes: Ratatouille 161
couscous: Barbecued pork chops with fennel, ginger
    and peach couscous 122
Celeriac, crispy bacon and parsley couscous risotto
    229
crabs: Crab, watercress, tomato and new potato hash
    48
    Simple velvet swimmer crab with pasta 187
Cranberry clementine compote 293
crisps: Sugar kelp crisps 53
    Winter veg crisps 267
cucumber: Smoked salmon with pickled cucumber 290

damper bread: Olive, rosemary and real ale damper
    bread 206–7
Darjeeling 93
**Duck breasts with ginger and orange with celeriac
    mash** 275

eggs: Asparagus, egg and baby leek salad with creamy
    dressing 82
    The breakfast burrito 225
    Parasol mushroom and rock samphire omelette 226
    Poached eggs with black pudding and sea beet 57
    Scrambled eggs with wild garlic 56
    Standby corned beef hash 266

fajitas: Family fajitas with a simple salsa 90–1
falafels: Fiery festival falafels with rocket and minty
    yoghurt 154
fennel: Barbecued pork chops with fennel, ginger and
    peach couscous 122
    Pork, scrumpy, apple and fennel pot roast 237
feta: Carrot and feta patties 81
fish: Barbecued fish parcels with lemon basil butter 126

Fish and chips 141
Fisherman's salad with summer salsa 163
Seafood laksa 234
smoking 183–4
see also individual fish
fondue: Cheese fondue 202
French onion soup with cheesy croutes 228

garlic: Moules with garlic butter 190
    Mussels in white wine and cream with wild garlic 47
    Sausages with white bean, garlic and sage mash 278
    Scrambled eggs with wild garlic 56
    Wild garlic pesto 58
ginger: Barbecued pork chops with fennel, ginger and
    peach couscous 122
    Duck breasts with ginger and orange with celeriac
    mash 275
    Lemon ginger squares 29
    Rhubarb and ginger martinis 89
Goat's cheese on toast with thyme and honey 77
green beans: Massaman chicken curry with beans and
    cashews 236
greengages: Poached greengages or apricots with
    lemon and lime cream 169

halloumi: Aubergine, pepper and halloumi kebabs with
    lemony houmous 128
harissa: Lentils with sweet potato, harissa and toasted
    seeds 269
hazelnuts: New potatoes with hazelnuts, mushrooms
    and crunch 157
houmous: Aubergine, pepper and halloumi kebabs with
    lemony houmous 128

jam: Tomato, chilli and mustard man jam 119

kebabs: Aubergine, pepper and halloumi kebabs with
    lemony houmous 128
    Curried pork kebabs 123
kelp: Sugar kelp crisps 53

lamb: Lamb gosht curry 272
    One pan lamb with peas, broad beans and mint 165
leeks: Asparagus, egg and baby leek salad with creamy
    dressing 82
Lemon Balm tea 281

lemons: Aubergine, pepper and halloumi kebabs with lemony houmous 128

Barbecued fish parcels with lemon basil butter 126

Joanne's Cally chicken with tarragon and lemon 164

Lemon ginger squares 29

Pan-fried sea trout with lemon parsley salsa 86

Parmesan and lemon popcorn 203

Poached greengages or apricots with lemon and lime cream 169

Lentils with sweet potato, harissa and toasted seeds 269

limes: Blackberry lime fizz 238

Poached greengages or apricots with lemon and lime cream 169

lobster: Barbecued lobster with Thai flavours 127

mackerel 177

Easy smoked mackerel pate on toast with radishes 185

Mackerel in newspaper 181

Mackerel with miso, soy and sesame 181

Mackerel with mustard caper butter 180

Mackerel with tomatoes, chorizo and fennel seed 180

Mackerel with a Vietnamese dressing 179

Maple and cinnamon popcorn 203

mayonnaise: Anchovy mayo 78

meatballs: Mart's meaty meatballs 92–3

mint: Fiery festival falafels with rocket and minty yoghurt 154

One pan lamb with peas, broad beans and mint 165

mojo dip: Canarian seawater spuds with a green mojo dip 158

Mulled honey pears 294

mushrooms: Aubergine and mushroom curry 233

New potatoes with hazelnuts, mushrooms and crunch 157

Parasol mushroom and rock samphire omelette 226

mussels: Moules in a foil parcel 191

Moules with garlic butter 190

Mussels in white wine and cream with wild garlic 47

Seafood laksa 234

mustard: mackerel with mustard caper butter 180

Tomato, chilli and mustard man jam 119

Nettle soup with crispy bacon 59

olives: Olive, rosemary and real ale damper bread 206–7

Sea bass with olives and capers 85

omelettes: Parasol mushroom and rock samphire omelette 226

onions: French onion soup with cheesy croutes 228

oranges: Duck breasts with ginger and orange with celeriac mash 275

Squid in minutes, with pepper, orange and chilli 124

Paella 166–7

pancakes 66

panettone: Pistachio and chocolate panettone Christmas cakes 296

Parasol mushroom and rock samphire omelette 226

parmesan: Cauliflower carbonara 79

Parmesan and lemon popcorn 203

Parmesan shortbreads 28

parsley: Celeriac, crispy bacon and parsley couscous risotto 229

Pan-fried sea trout with lemon parsley salsa 86

Root veggies with chestnuts and parsley 293

parsnips: Root veggies with chestnuts and parsley 293

Winter veg crisps 267

peaches: Barbecued pork chops with fennel, ginger and peach couscous 122

pears: Mulled honey pears 294

Spiced perry 281

peas: One pan lamb with peas, broad beans and mint 165

Peppermint tea 171

peppers: Aubergine, pepper and halloumi kebabs with lemony houmous 128

Ratatouille 161

Roasted pepper salsa 78

Squid in minutes, with pepper, orange and chilli 124

pesto: Wild garlic pesto 58

Pistachio and chocolate panettone Christmas cakes 296

pizza: Frying pan mini pizzas 204

pollock: Fish and chips 141

popcorn 203

pork: Barbecued pork chops with fennel, ginger and peach couscous 122

Curried pork kebabs 123

Pork, scrumpy, apple and fennel pot roast 237

see also bacon; chorizo; sausages

potatoes: The breakfast burrito 225

Canarian seawater spuds with a green mojo dip 158
Chunky colcannon 69
Crab, watercress, tomato and new potato hash 48
New potatoes with hazelnuts, mushrooms and crunch 157
Poor man's potatoes 268
Root veggies with chestnuts and parsley 293
prawns: Campervan paella 166–7
Fisherman's salad with summer salsa 163
Seafood laksa 234
Purple sprouting with two extras 78

radishes: Easy smoked mackerel pate on toast with radishes 105
New potatoes with hazelnuts, mushrooms and crunch 157
raspberries: Raspberry and banana traybake with cinnamon crumble topping 32
Strawberries and raspberries with zesty sugar 171
Ratatouille 161
red peppers *see peppers*
rhubarb: Rhubarb and custard pots 94
Rhubarb and ginger martinis 89
rice: Campervan paella 166–7
Cheat's nutmeggy rice pud with jam 279
Spring to summer risotto 84
Thermos rice pudding 34
risotto: Celeriac, crispy bacon and parsley couscous risotto 229
Spring to summer risotto 84
rock samphire: Parasol mushroom and rock samphire omelette 226
rocket: Fiery festival falafels with rocket and minty yoghurt 154
Rocky road bananas 130
rosemary: Olive, rosemary and real ale damper bread 206–7

sage: Sausages with white bean, garlic and sage mash 278
Turkey with 'sage stuffing' crumbs 292
salmon: Smoked salmon with pickled cucumber 290
salsa: Family fajitas with a simple salsa 90–1
Fisherman's salad with summer salsa 163
Pan-fried sea trout with lemon parsley salsa 86
Roasted pepper salsa 78

Sausages with white bean, garlic and sage mash 278
scallops: Fisherman's salad with summer salsa 163
Scallops with garam masala butter 88
sea bass: Sea bass with olives and capers 85
Sea bass with a simple fresh tomato and basil sauce 139
sea beet: Poached eggs with black pudding and sea beet 57
sea trout: Pan-fried sea trout with lemon parsley salsa 86
seafood: Fisherman's salad with summer salsa 163
Seafood laksa 234
see also individual seafood
seaweed 50–3
shortbread: Parmesan shortbreads 28
sprouts: Essential buttery sprouts 293
Squid in minutes, with pepper, orange and chilli 124
Steak and chips 230
strawberries: Strawberries and raspberries with zesty sugar 171
Strawberry 'mess' 170
Sugar kelp crisps 53
sweet potatoes: Lentils with sweet potato, harissa and toasted seeds 269

tarragon: Joanne's Cally chicken with tarragon and lemon 164
tea 35, 93, 171, 238, 281
thyme: Goat's cheese on toast with thyme and honey 77
tomatoes: Crab, watercress, tomato and new potato hash 48
mackerel with tomatoes, chorizo and fennel seed 180
Ratatouille 161
Sea bass with a simple fresh tomato and basil sauce 139
Tomato, chilli and mustard man jam 119
trout: Pan-fried sea trout with lemon parsley salsa 86
Turkey with 'sage stuffing' crumbs 292
turnips: Winter veg crisps 267

velvet swimmer crab: Simple velvet swimmer crab with pasta 187

watercress: Crab, watercress, tomato and new potato hash 48
Welsh rarebit with real ale 276

First published in Great Britain in 2012 by Saltyard Books
An imprint of Hodder & Stoughton
An Hachette UK company

1

Text © Martin Dorey 2012
Recipes © Sarah Randell 2012
Recipes marked with ◀ © Martin Dorey 2012

Photography © Martin Dorey 2012
Other photographs © 2012 by:
Georgia Glynn Smith pages 6, 30, 33, 49, 80, 83, 87, 95, 119, 123,
129, 158, 160, 166, 231, 232, 235, 239, 271, 277, 291 and 295
Nico Chapman pages 24, 35, 37, 41, 54, 55, 57, 77, 115, 136, 140,
143, 149, 150, 153, 157, 174, 193, 215, 216, 222, 252, 268 and 273
Dave Lamacraft page 76
Maggie Dorey page 134
Simon Mitchell page 142
Gary McCall page 251

A CIP catalogue record for this title is available from the British Library.

978 1 444 703 94 8

Design and page make-up by Craig Burgess
Food and props stylist Polly Webb-Wilson
Copy editor Zelda Turner
Proofreader Margaret Gilby
Indexer Caroline Wilding

Printed and bound in China by C&C Offset Printing Co Ltd

Hodder & Stoughton policy is to use papers that are natural, renewable and recyclable products
and made from wood grown in sustainable forests. The logging and manufacturing processes
are expected to conform to the environmental regulations of the country of origin.

Hodder & Stoughton Ltd
338 Euston Road
London NW1 3BH

www.saltyardbooks.co.uk